THE EARLY 20TH CENTURY

Edited by Tim Cooke

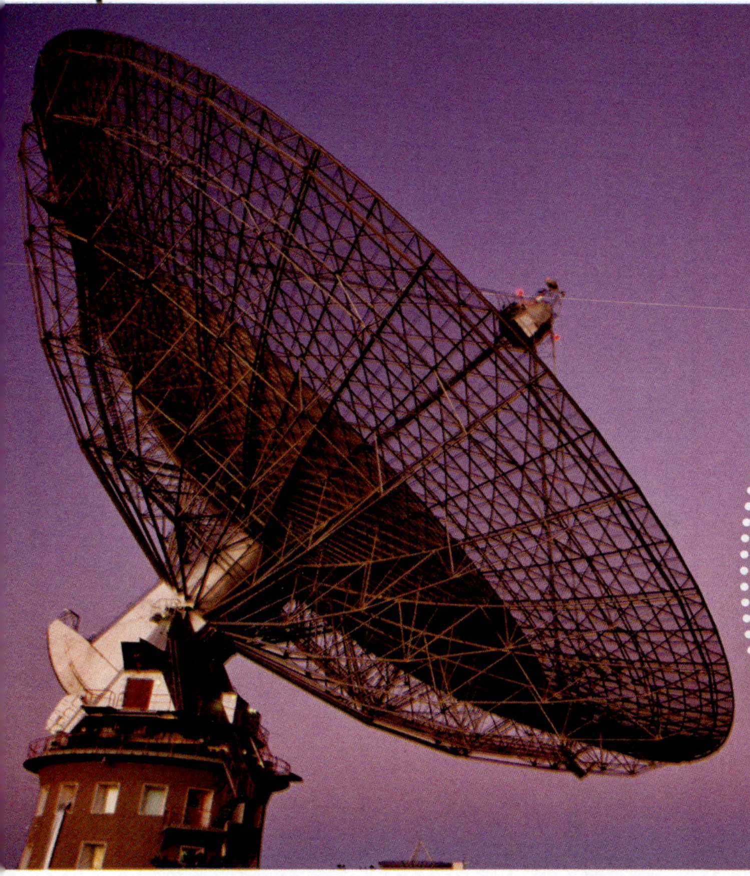

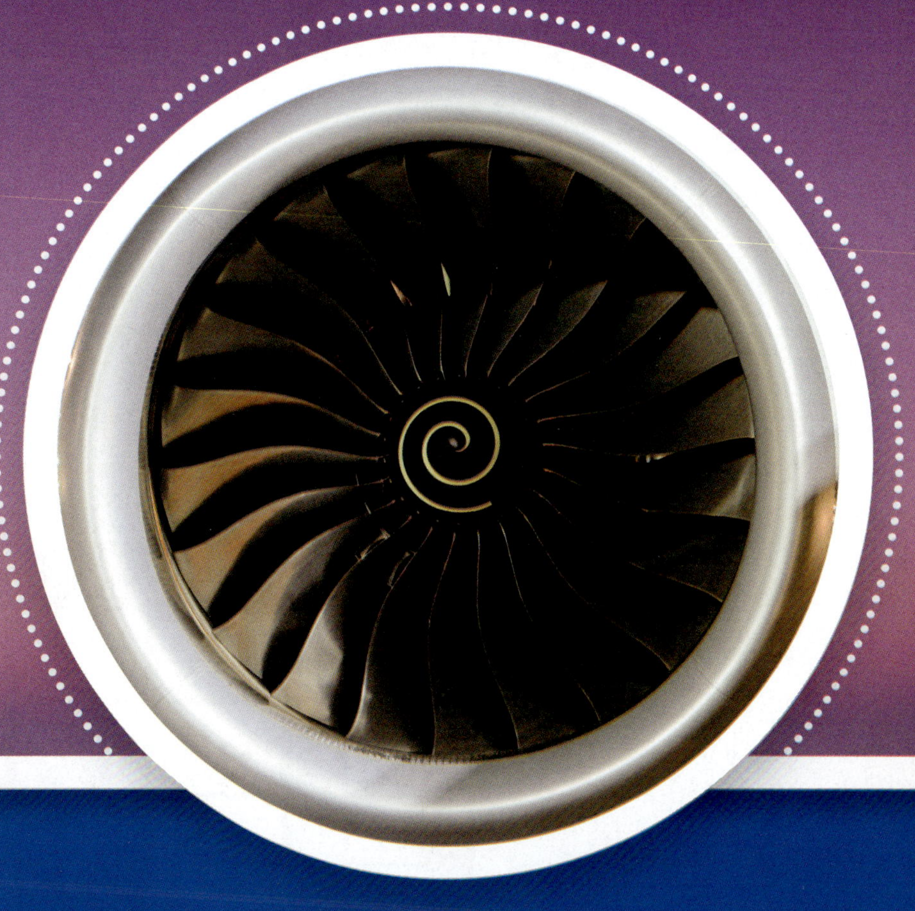

TEACHER RESOURCES

SCIENTIFIC DISCOVERY

LIGHTBOX
openlightbox.com

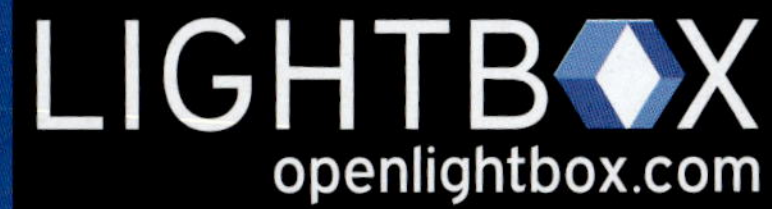

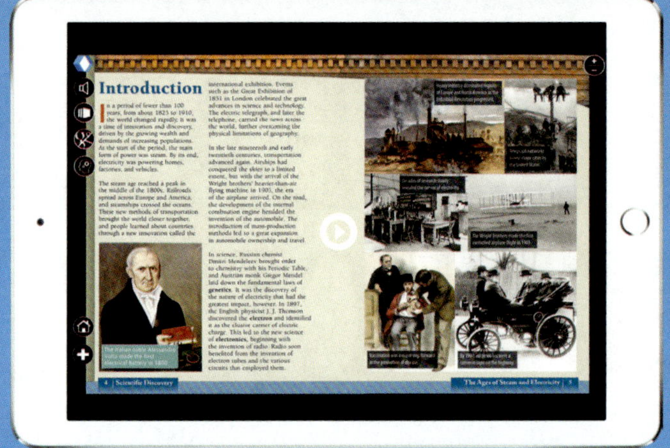

Lightbox is an all-inclusive digital solution for the teaching and learning of curriculum topics in an original, groundbreaking way. Lightbox is based on National Curriculum Standards.

STANDARD FEATURES OF LIGHTBOX

 **AUDIO** High-quality narration using text-to-speech system

 **VIDEOS** Embedded high-definition video clips

ACTIVITIES Printable PDFs that can be emailed and graded

 **WEBLINKS** Curated links to external, child-safe resources

 **SLIDESHOWS** Pictorial overviews of key concepts

TRANSPARENCIES Step-by-step layering of maps, diagrams, charts, and timelines

 **INTERACTIVE MAPS** Interactive maps and aerial satellite imagery

 **QUIZZES** Ten multiple choice questions that are automatically graded and emailed for teacher assessment

 **KEY WORDS** Matching key concepts to their definitions

 **MORE** Extra information and details on the subject

 **FIRST HAND** Letters, diaries, and other primary sources

 **DOCS** Speeches, newspaper articles, and other historical documents

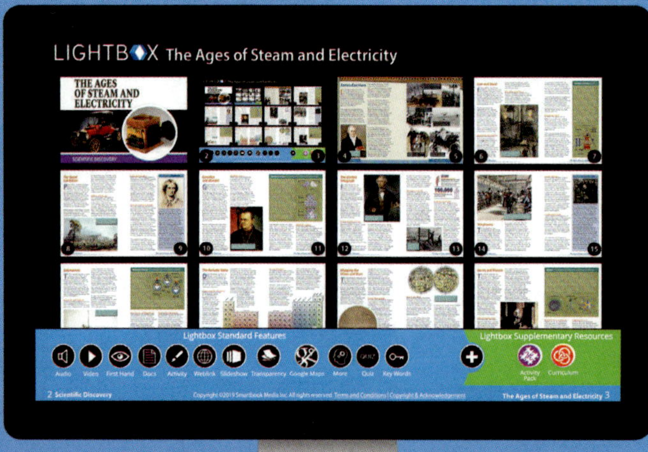

Contents

Introduction

The period from about 1910 to 1959 saw many advances in science and technology. Research and innovation were influenced most significantly by two major conflicts. Scientists were recruited by governments to improve weapons, transportation, industry, and medicine during World War I (1914–1818) and, more particularly, World War II (1939–1945).

The new science of electronics continued to expand, first with the invention of television and then with the development of radar. After the end of World War I, some military radars were converted to radio telescopes, and the new science of radio astronomy was established. After World War II, the invention of the transistor and the laser revolutionized the electronics industry, accelerating development of the computer and other electronic devices that are widely taken for granted today. Alongside the rapid advances in conventional aircraft, including jet engines, World War II encouraged the development of the helicopter. The war also concentrated efforts on rocket research, particularly in Germany.

The development of warplanes led to the development of better anti-aircraft weapons.

One beneficial outcome of the conflict was the development of methods of mass-producing the antibiotic penicillin, which was needed in large quantities to treat the wounded. The discovery of penicillin by Alexander Fleming in 1928 had added a new weapon to the war against disease. That battle had already progressed earlier in the century with the synthesis of new drugs based on natural materials.

The first half of the twentieth century was also defined by research into the structure of the atom. This ultimately led to the discovery of nuclear fission, itself the precursor to the detonation of the atomic bombs that were unleashed on Japan in 1945. The new science of molecular biology also emerged. The most famous advance in the field was the understanding of the double helix structure of the deoxyribonucleic acid (DNA) molecule, the means by which parents pass on characteristics to their offspring.

Electronic computers gave an idea of the potential of computing for helping to process information.

Television and radio revolutionized mass communication.

Innovations such as jet aircraft were encouraged by the two world wars.

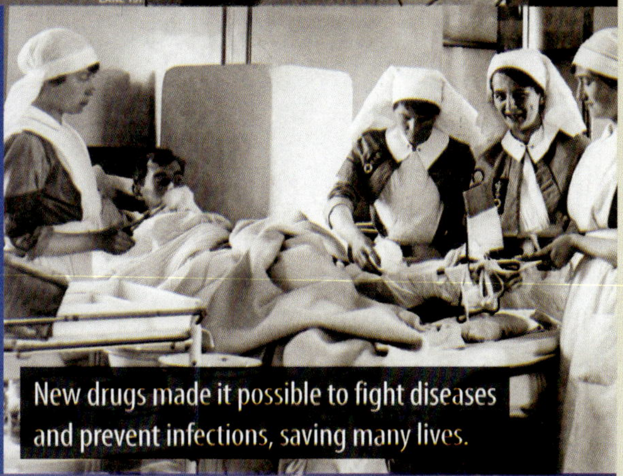

New drugs made it possible to fight diseases and prevent infections, saving many lives.

In the early 1900s, theories were put forward about the structure of the atom.

Radio telescopes added to astronomers' growing realization of the size and age of the universe.

ACTIVITIES

Video

The History of Jet Engines

Examine and assess the history of jet engines.

1. Who were the first scientists to develop a successful jet engine? Why were they developed?
2. What improvements were made to jet engines after World War II? Summarize the history of jet-engine aircraft since 1950.
3. Why is the ratio of the speed of an airplane to the speed of sound called the Mach number?

Weblink

History of Technology

Analyze the rise of science and technology in the early twentieth century.

1. What were the key scientific developments in the aftermath of World Wars I and II? Which discovery might have been the most significant? What other discoveries could be added to the list? Justify your answer.
2. The post-war periods saw economic hardships in many countries, particularly in Europe, yet despite this, the early twentieth century witnessed more advances in science and technology than had been recorded in previous centuries. Why do you think this might have been? Analyze what might be key drivers for developments in scientific research today. Explain and defend your responses.

RUBRIC

Sketching a Design Solution

As a group, brainstorm possible engineering design solutions for a new type of bicycle. Select the best design and make a sketch of a model or prototype. An exemplary project will meet the following criteria:

- The problem is defined in detail
- All constraints are listed
- Possible solutions from the brainstorming session are listed
- Two or three ideas are selected from brainstormed list
- Sketches are created for the selected idea
- Sketches are labeled with dimensions and materials for each component
- Detailed list of materials is included
- Detailed procedures are included
- Hypothesis following an "if..., then..." format is developed for the design
- Strengths of the design are listed
- Weaknesses of the design or compromises of the design are listed
- The chosen design effectively addresses the identified problem
- Modifications to the design are documented
- Presentation is well-organized
- Presentation is clearly communicated visually with appropriate data, sketches, graphs or pictures
- Presentation includes contributions from all team members

The Bicycle

In the 1860s, a French invalid carriage-maker called Pierre Lallement attached pedals and cranks to the front wheel of a two-wheeled bicycle, or bike, to create a machine that could be powered by a its riders. The new velocipede began a craze. Training schools opened to teach the growing numbers of riders. The first race for velocipedes was held near Paris on May 31, 1868. The following year a race was held over 83 miles (134 km) between Paris and Rouen.

The Penny Farthing

In the 1870s, a bicycle evolved in which the rider towered above a high front wheel, steering with almost vertical forks. The frame of the bike was a simple metal tube that followed the curve of the front wheel. It attached to a tiny wheel at the back. The machine was called the Ordinary because it was accepted as being the standard design of the time, but it also acquired the nickname of "penny farthing" because its wheels looked like large and small coins of the day. The most popular design of the Ordinary was named the Ariel. Designed by Englishman James Starley, the machine was improved over the next 20 years. Despite the popularity of the Ordinary, many people found it difficult to ride. Even expert riders would often injure themselves when they were thrown over the handlebars.

Many people tried to build safer bicycles. These machines used chains or levers to gear-up a smaller front wheel so that one turn of the pedals made the bicycle wheel turn more than once. Eventually, the popularity of these machines, called safety bicycles, led to the rapid disappearance of the Ordinary.

The Ordinary was so high that it was difficult to get on and off the seat.

In a safety bicycle, gears transmit rotary motion to the back wheel via the chain.

New Bicycles

The machine that changed the shape of bicycles forever was called the Rover Safety. It was introduced in 1885 by the nephew of James Starley, John Kemp Starley. The Rover Safety set the shape of modern bicycles. The rear wheel was driven by a chain, and a strong frame replaced the single tube used on the Ordinary.

Other companies manufactured their own safetys. Wheels became equal-sized, the diamond-shaped frame was introduced, and finally the air-filled **pneumatic tire** was added. This was invented in 1888 by John Boyd Dunlop, when he fitted canvas-covered sheet rubber tubes to his son's three-wheeled tricycle. By the turn of the century, the safety was the standard form of the bicycle, and it has only changed in small detail since.

Derailleur Gears

Derailleur gears were invented in 1911. They consist of cogs attached to the drive shaft of the rear wheel, and a tension pinion that moves the chain. A cable connects the tension pinion to the gear lever. On a flat surface, a high gear is selected, and the tension pinion moves the chain to a small cog. One turn of the pedals rotates the wheel several times. On a hill, however, the cyclist selects a larger cog. The bike moves less distance for each turn of the pedals, but the effort is less.

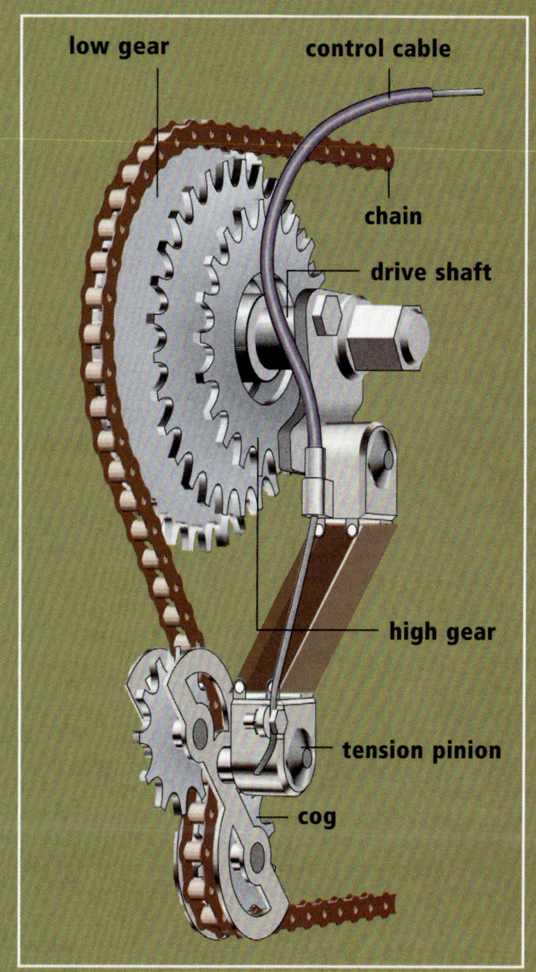

ACTIVITIES

Transparency

Derailleur Gears

Evaluate the merits of the derailleur gear system.

1. Describe the main difference between cycles with and without derailleur gear systems. What does the French word "derailleur" mean?
2. What are the main advantages of derailleur gears? Explain in your own words what is happening in the diagram.

Weblink

James Starley. Inventor and Father of the Bicycle Industry

Analyze the path taken by James Starley in his development of the Ordinary.

1. Who invented the velocipede that inspired Starley to produce his own bicycle design? Why was the velocipede nicknamed the "boneshaker?"
2. Why were the successors to the velocipede called "penny farthings"? Explain the technological advancements of Starley's version of the penny farthing over French boneshakers.
3. Explain how the Rover Safety set the shape of modern bicycle design. Assess how this design has changed since it was first introduced.

Synthetic Drugs

Humans have used naturally occurring substances as medicines for thousands of years. Some of them, such as opiates, were used as analgesics, or painkillers. They were never very reliable, and they often had undesirable side effects on the patient, such as making him or her unconscious.

Anesthetics

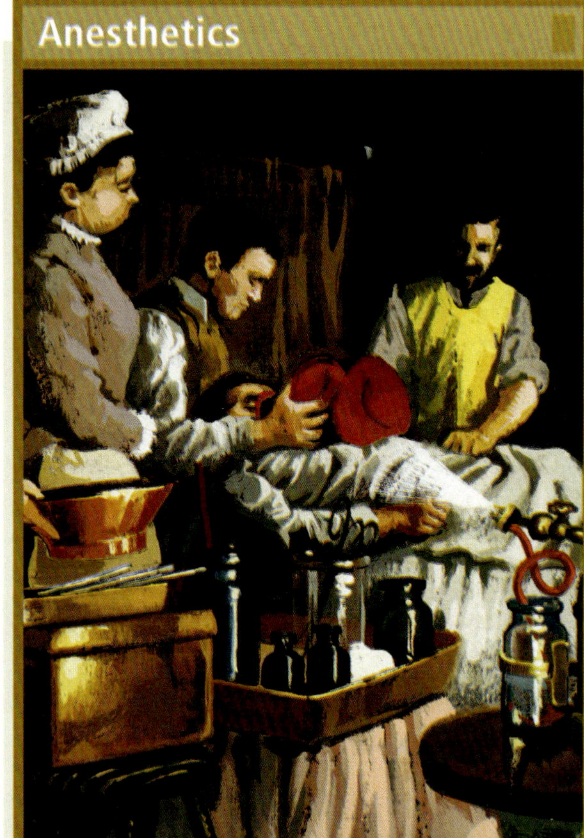

When invented: 1847

Where invented: Edinburgh, Scotland

Inventor: James Simpson

Active ingredient: Chloroform

Advantages: Aided women in childbirth by reducing pain

Drawbacks: Made patients unconscious, poisonous in large quantities

Painkillers

When invented: 1888

Where invented: Elberfeld, Germany

Inventor: Bayer Company

Active ingredients: Acetanilide, phenacetin

Advantages: Effective painkiller, reduced fever

Drawbacks: Excessive use could cause cancers

The first wholly synthetic drugs were gases. In 1799, English chemist Humphry Davy discovered the painkilling properties of nitrous oxide, also known as laughing gas. In 1815, similar properties were noted for ether vapor. The gases were administered via a mask over the patient's mouth.

Aspirin

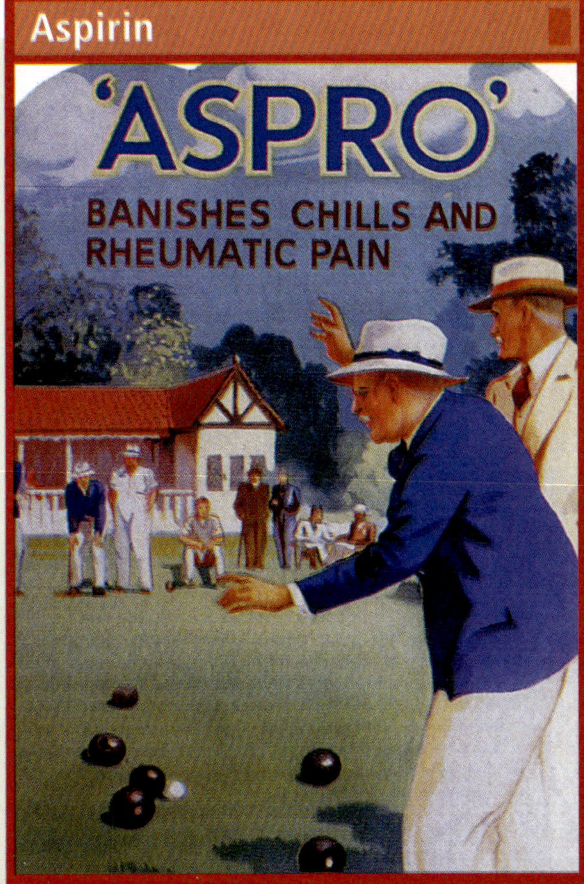

When invented: 1899
Where invented: Elberfeld, Germany
Inventor: Felix Hoffman
Active ingredient: Salicylic acid
Advantages: Effective painkiller
Drawbacks: Could damage stomach in large quantities

Salvarsan

When invented: 1906
Where invented: Frankfurt, Germany
Inventor: Paul Ehrlich
Active ingredient: Arsenic
Advantages: Combatted specific diseases
Drawbacks: Required a long course of treatment

More

Synthetic Drugs
Compare and contrast four of the first synthetic drugs and determine their value in the evolution of synthetic drugs.

1. Compare the four drugs. Assess each one for advantages and disadvantages when used to combat pain.
2. Which of the four anesthetics has been the most significant for future developments in the field? Why is this the case?

RUBRIC

Developing a Presentation on a Well-Known Structure

Create a PowerPoint presentation to teach your class about the building of the Panama Canal. An exemplary PowerPoint presentation will meet the following criteria:

- Includes information about the function and style highlights of the structure
- Describes the main materials used and explains the reason for their selection
- Explains safety considerations that the structure's design took into account
- Includes appropriate photographs of the structure and credits the photographers
- Delivers the message in a confident, poised, and enthusiastic fashion
- Varies the volume and rate to add emphasis and interest
- Uses clear pronunciation and enunciation
- Exhibits very few filler words, such as "ahs," "uhms," or "you knows,"
- Helps the listener understand the sequence and relationships of ideas by using organizational aids such as announcing the topic, previewing the organization, using transitions, and summarizing
- Presents material in a very original way to capture the audience's attention
- Uses visual aids appropriately to add interest and clarify concepts

The Panama Canal

The Panama Canal connects the Atlantic and Pacific Oceans. It eliminates the need for a 6,000-mile (10,000-km) journey around the tip of South America through treacherous waters. Soon after the Spanish conquered and explored Central America in the sixteenth century, they saw the advantages of a canal across the **Isthmus** of Panama. Engineers drew up various plans in the 1530s. However, neither the Spanish government nor the new Central American republics took any action until the United States funded the construction of the Panama Railroad across the isthmus in the mid-nineteenth century. In 1878, the government of Colombia granted a concession to an international company to dig a canal.

French engineer and diplomat Ferdinand de Lesseps had gained a worldwide reputation as a canal builder after completing the Suez Canal in 1869. Led by de Lesseps, a new company, the Compagnie Universelle du Canal Interocéanique, began work on the Panama Canal in 1881. Poor planning and the deaths of many workers from disease forced the company into bankruptcy.

Large ships have little clearance as they pass through paired canal locks such as those at Miraflores.

A second attempt in 1894 also failed, and construction stopped in 1898. In 1902, the U.S. government bought the remnants of the company. A year later, it signed a treaty with the new state of Panama for a permanent lease on a 10-mile (16-km) strip of land, the Panama Canal Zone.

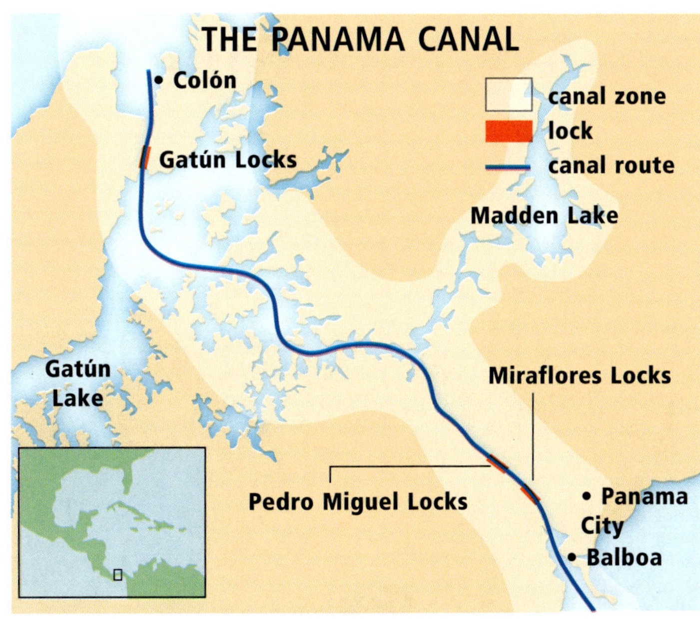

The route of the canal was designed to follow the paths of natural rivers as far as possible.

A Daring Plan

Work on the canal restarted in 1904, spurred on by the enthusiasm of U.S. presidents Theodore Roosevelt and William Howard Taft. It was decided to build a canal with **locks**, following a plan drawn up in 1879 by French engineer Adolphe de Brusly. A daring part of the plan included the great earth dam across the Chagres River to create Gatún Lake.

The work on the canal was carried out by the U.S. Army Corps of Engineers. Their commander, Colonel George Goethals, later became governor of the Canal Zone. Colonel William Gorgas of the U.S. Army Medical Corps sanitized the area to eliminate the mosquitoes that carried and spread disease among the workers.

Canal Statistics

The canal was the greatest engineering undertaking since the building of the pyramids of Egypt. With the help of steam shovels, up to 40,000 workers dug out about 5,120 million cubic feet (145 million cubic meters) of earth. Excavated channels big enough to take ocean-going ships run for about two-thirds of the canal's 40-mile (64-kilometers) length. There are three paired locks at the Gatún Locks, giving a total lift of 85 feet (25.9 m). Another pair of locks, the Pedro Miguel Locks, provide a drop of 31 feet (9.4 m), and two more pairs at Miraflores give a final drop of 51 feet (15.5 m). The work was completed in 1914, at an estimated cost of $336 million.

Reverting Control

Under a 1977 treaty with Panama, the United States retained military bases near the canal. All the land and water in the former Panama Canal Zone reverted to Panama. At the end of 1999, control of the Panama Canal itself also reverted to the government of Panama.

ACTIVITIES

Video

Panama Canal Construction, 1912

Analyze the process that led to the construction of the Panama Canal.

1. Why did early attempts to construct the Panama Canal fail? Assess the dangers the workers would have encountered at the time they were digging the canal. Would workers today be allowed to work in such conditions? Summarize your conclusions.
2. Why was the Panama Canal built with locks? Explain why it was not dug so that it was at sea level. Why is the Panama Canal considered to be one of the Seven Wonders of the Modern World? Justify the description.

Weblink

The History and Future of the Panama Canal

Assess the value of the Panama Canal in relation to the costs involved in its creation.

1. Why was the location of the Panama Canal chosen? Why did the United States government take control of the project in 1902?
2. How much did it cost the government to build the canal? Was the cost of the canal outweighed by the benefits to trade once the canal finally opened? Justify your conclusions.
3. What impact, both positive and negative, did the construction of the canal have on the local people and surrounding area?
4. What factors might determine the future of the Panama Canal? Justify your conclusions.

The Machine Gun

A machine gun is a small-caliber weapon that keeps firing as long as the trigger is held down. A machine gun has a mechanism that automatically carries out a cycle of loading, firing, and extracting cartridge cases. The term applies to an automatic carbine or rifle. Handguns of this type are called machine pistols.

Gatling Gun

When invented: 1862

Inventor: Richard Gatling

Rate of fire: 350 rounds per minute

Barrels: 10

Crew: 4

Advantages: High rate of fire, long range

Drawbacks: Liable to jam, not very maneuverable on original carriage, required more than one man to operate

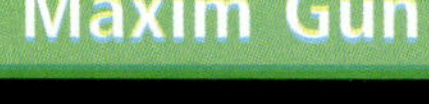

Maxim Gun

When invented: 1883

Inventor: Hiram Maxim

Rate of fire: 600 rounds per minute

Barrels: 1

Crew: 4

Advantages: High rate of fire, self-loading action, rarely jammed

Drawbacks: Tendency to overheat, water jacket made gun very heavy

ACTIVITIES

The first multiple-firing cannon was patented in 1718, by English lawyer James Puckle. Its cylinder had 10 chambers, and was rotated by hand. In 1856, Charles Barnes in the United States added a crank to rotate the cylinder and work the breech automatically. The gun could fire up to 80 rounds per minute.

Light Machine Gun

When invented: 1902

Inventor: Newton Lewis (Lewis gun, 1911)

Rate of fire: 550 rounds per minute

Barrels: 1

Crew: 1

Advantages: Air-cooled barrel allowed high rate of fire

Drawbacks: Heavy to carry, although it could be operated by one man

Submachine Gun

When invented: 1918

Inventor: John Thompson (Tommy gun, 1920)

Rate of fire: 500–800 rounds per minute

Barrels: 1

Crew: 1

Advantages: Light to carry and use, cheap to manufacture

Drawbacks: Limited range, not effective against body armor

More

The Machine Gun

Analyze the development of the machine gun and its uses in the past and present.

1. How did the machine gun evolve over time? Which changes were the most beneficial to soldiers? Why?
2. Which machine gun has had the most significant effect on modern warfare? Why?

RUBRIC

Creating a Scientific Drawing

Create a scientific drawing of three different atoms from different parts of the periodic table. An exemplary scientific drawing will meet the following criteria:

- Includes a descriptive an accurate title
- Accurately depicts the atoms
- Draws on multiple perspectives to provide the viewer with a complete picture
- Clearly labels all parts of the scientific drawing with the correct terms
- Includes a written explanation of the drawing
- Provides a key or legend

Subatomic Particles

By 1920, physicists knew that atoms consist of a nucleus carrying a positive electromagnetic charge, surrounded by a cloud of electrons carrying a negative charge. This implies that the atom is not an "elementary particle," which cannot be divided into smaller constituents. Before long, scientists were identifying a growing list of particles much smaller than atoms.

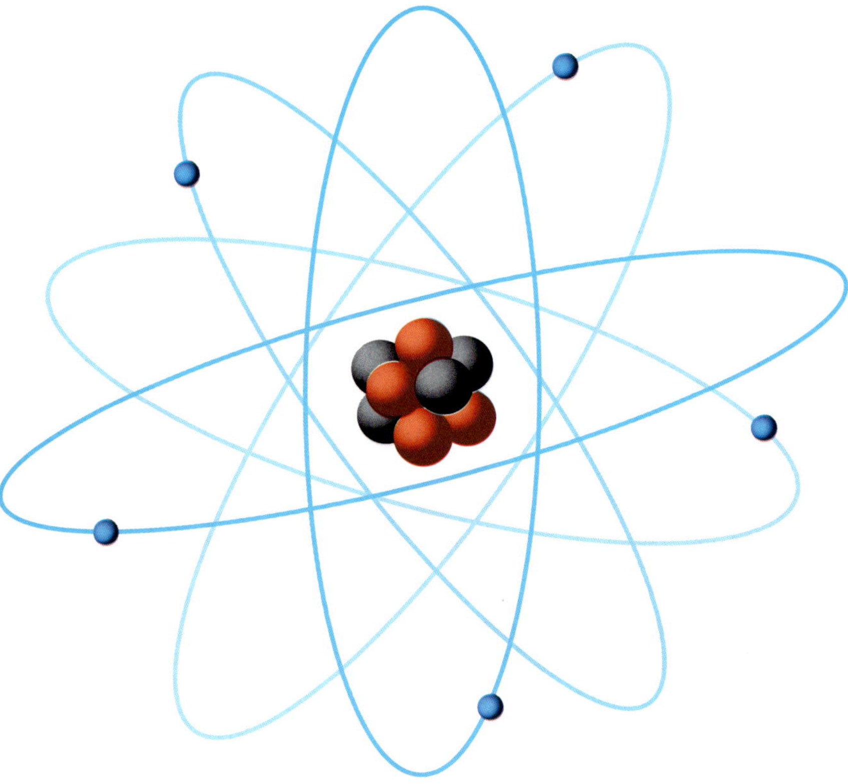

Rutherford's atomic model proposed a nucleus that was surrounded by orbiting electrons.

Smashing Atoms

Ernest Rutherford, a New Zealand-born English physicist working at the Cavendish Laboratory in Cambridge, found that bombarding nitrogen atoms with alpha particles, or helium nuclei, released hydrogen nuclei. It followed that a nitrogen atomic nucleus must contain hydrogen nuclei. In 1920, Rutherford suggested the name "proton" for the hydrogen nucleus. It came from the Greek word *protos*, meaning "first." The mass of a proton is 1,836.12 times that of an electron, and the mass of an atom is effectively the mass of its nucleus. In the same year, Rutherford suggested that the nuclei of atoms more massive than hydrogen also contain particles carrying no electromagnetic charge.

A New Form of Radiation

During the 1920s in Berlin, German physicist Walther Bothe led a team of scientists investigating the atom. They fired alpha particles at atoms of certain light elements, including beryllium, boron, and lithium. In 1930, they discovered that this bombardment resulted in the emission of highly penetrating radiation. At first, the scientists thought this was gamma radiation, although they noticed that it was more penetrative than any gamma radiation known at the time. In 1934, French physicists Irène and Frédéric Joliot-Curie carried out their own similar experiments.

They fired alpha particles at paraffins or similar hydrocarbons, which are compounds of hydrogen and carbon. This alpha bombardment resulted in the emission of protons with very high energy. Closer study of this phenomenon made it increasingly unlikely that what Bothe and his colleagues had observed was in fact the emission of gamma radiation.

Discovering the Neutron

English physicist James Chadwick worked alongside Rutherford at the Cavendish Laboratory. He finally conducted experiments proving that the emission the German team had identified could not have been gamma radiation. He suggested instead that the radiation consisted of particles that had about the same mass as the proton, but which carried no electromagnetic charge.

Chadwick suspected the new particle was a proton bound to an electron. When he bombarded boron, an element of known relative atomic mass, he was able to calculate the mass of the particle. The mass turned out to be 1.0087 atomic mass units, making it slightly more massive than the proton (1.007276 a.m.u.). The particle carries no charge, so it was named the "**neutron**." A neutron is stable while it remains inside an atomic nucleus. Outside the nucleus, however, a neutron decays into a proton, an electron, and an antineutrino. Protons and neutrons, the constituents of atomic nuclei, are known as "nucleons."

Particle Acceleration

Ernest Rutherford became professor of physics at Cambridge University and director of the Cavendish Laboratory in 1919. His research centered on smashing atomic nuclei by bombarding them with alpha particles. In 1925, English physicist Patrick Blackett, working under Rutherford's direction, improved the cloud chamber. This device had been invented in 1911 by Scottish physicist C.T.R. Wilson. Blackett used it for recording the disintegration of atoms. Alpha particles were not powerful enough to smash large nuclei, however, which repelled them without disintegrating. More energetic impacts were needed, and in 1932 English physicist John Cockcroft and his Irish colleague Ernest Walton built the world's first particle accelerator at the Cavendish Laboratory. It used powerful electromagnets to accelerate protons that were then directed at a target. The particle accelerator became the key tool in subatomic research.

ACTIVITIES

First Hand

Atom Man

Evaluate the life and achievements of Ernest Rutherford.

1. Rutherford famously said of his upbringing in rural New Zealand, "We don't have the money, so we have to think." How did his background in New Zealand have an impact on how Rutherford went about his scientific research?
2. What impact did Rutherford's three major discoveries have on science? How would the world be different if these discoveries had not taken place?

Weblink

What Is An Atom?

Analyze arguments regarding the mass of an atom.

1. Do electrons have a mass or are they just an electric charge? Review the arguments about the mass of an electron.
2. How big is the space within the shell of electrons of an atom relative to the size of the nucleus? Describe whether protons are bigger or smaller than neutrons.

RUBRIC

Researching for a Writing Assignment

Students will complete a thorough research process to prepare for a writing assignment on the history of television, and organize their research in a logical manner that supports their writing. An exemplary research process will meet the following criteria:

- Creates a goal for the research, based on the topic and working thesis
- Creates specific, thoughtful, and inventive research questions that are relevant to the topic of the writing assignment
- Produces a list of categories, key words, and related ideas to effectively assist in researching
- Uses high-quality sources that pertain to the topic and come in a variety of formats, such as books, journals, primary sources, websites, and databases
- Uses sources that provide balanced research and various perspectives of the topic in question
- Takes notes to highlight the key facts and ideas in order to answer all research questions
- Extracts relevant, detailed information from the sources
- Writes notes in the student's own words
- Organizes the research notes in a clear and concise manner
- Analyzes the information and produces ideas and points to support the working thesis
- Uses an effective and suitable format to present all research
- Properly cites all sources used
- Uses quotations properly and ethically

Television

In October 1925, the Scottish electrical engineer John Logie Baird transmitted the first television pictures in his London workshop. This first camera and receiver were basically mechanical in operation. In the United States, Vladimir Zworykin later developed an electronic system on which modern TV technology is still largely based.

John Logie Baird was born in the west of Scotland and educated in Glasgow. He was excused from military service at the start of World War I (1914–1918) because of poor health, which also cost him his job as an electrical engineer. After three failed businesses, he retired to live in the southern English coastal town of Hastings in 1922. It was there that he began experimenting with television.

Pictures Through a Disk

A television works by duplicating moving images as a series of horizontal lines on a screen. To scan a subject as a series of lines, Baird used a rapidly spinning Nipkow disk, patented by German electrical engineer Paul Nipkow in 1884. An observer looking through the disk sees a series of lines, each produced by a different hole in the disk. Baird used the disk to scan the first TV pictures in 1925, depicting a ventriloquist's doll named Stooky Bill. The first live subject, in 1926, was an office boy from the premises below Baird's London workshop.

The Nipkow disk is pierced with a spiral of holes that scans an image as a series of curved lines.

John Logie Baird is often called the inventor of television, but the device required contributions from many inventors.

At first, Baird sent, or transmitted, his television images along wires. His “noctovisor” method used **infrared rays** for the scanning process, so that it captured images in the dark. By 1927, Baird had transmitted pictures from London to Glasgow along a telephone line. A year later, he sent pictures over the Atlantic telegraph cable to New York City, and also to a ship in the Atlantic Ocean.

The First TV Broadcasts

In September 1929, the British Broadcasting Corporation (BBC) began experimental broadcasts using Baird’s mechanical system. The flickering images consisted of only 30 lines, later increased to 60, and eventually 240 lines. In 1932, Baird transmitted moving images by short-wave radio. The experimental broadcasts ended in 1935. By the time commercial television broadcasting really started in Great Britain in 1937, the BBC had adopted the 405-line electronic system developed by the British company Marconi-EMI. TV broadcasting was soon suspended for the duration of World War II (1939–1945). However, before the end of the conflict, Baird had produced color television and three-dimensional images. He also developed a widescreen system and stereophonic sound. Baird died before TV broadcasting resumed. When it started again, Baird’s mechanical process had been abandoned in favor of the all-electronic system developed in the United States.

ACTIVITIES

Video

Television 1939 RCA: An Early Introduction to TV

Examine the development of the television and its impact on the American public.

1. What impact did the development of the television initially have on the general public in the United States? How did this change over time? What circumstances led to these changes?
2. Which company dominated the radio business before the advent of television in the United States? What effect did this have on the development of electronic television over mechanical television in the United States?

Weblink

John Logie Baird

Analyze the context under which John Logie Baird developed his mechanical television system.

1. What was the starting point for Baird’s mechanical television system? How did Baird’s system evolve from that point?
2. Who were the other pioneers working on television at the same time as Baird? What system were they using, and how did it differ from Baird’s system? Which of these pioneers had the greater impact on the further development of television? How?

Rockets

In July 1969, a huge Saturn V rocket carried three U.S. astronauts to the Moon. The technology that made this possible had its origins nearly eight centuries before. From the 1100s, the Chinese used rockets both for ornamental fireworks and as weapons of war. Knowledge of rockets quickly spread to Europe, and in 1288, the Moors used them to attack Valencia in Spain. The earliest European drawing of a rocket is in a military manual from about 1400. Multistage rockets, with one section mounted on top of another, came next. In 1806, the English military engineer William Congreve started making rockets with an explosive warhead. Some Congreve rockets reached targets 1.5 miles (2.5 km) away. They were employed as artillery in the Napoleonic Wars (1799–1815). Rocket technology advanced rapidly in the first half of the twentieth century thanks to a series of visionaries around the world.

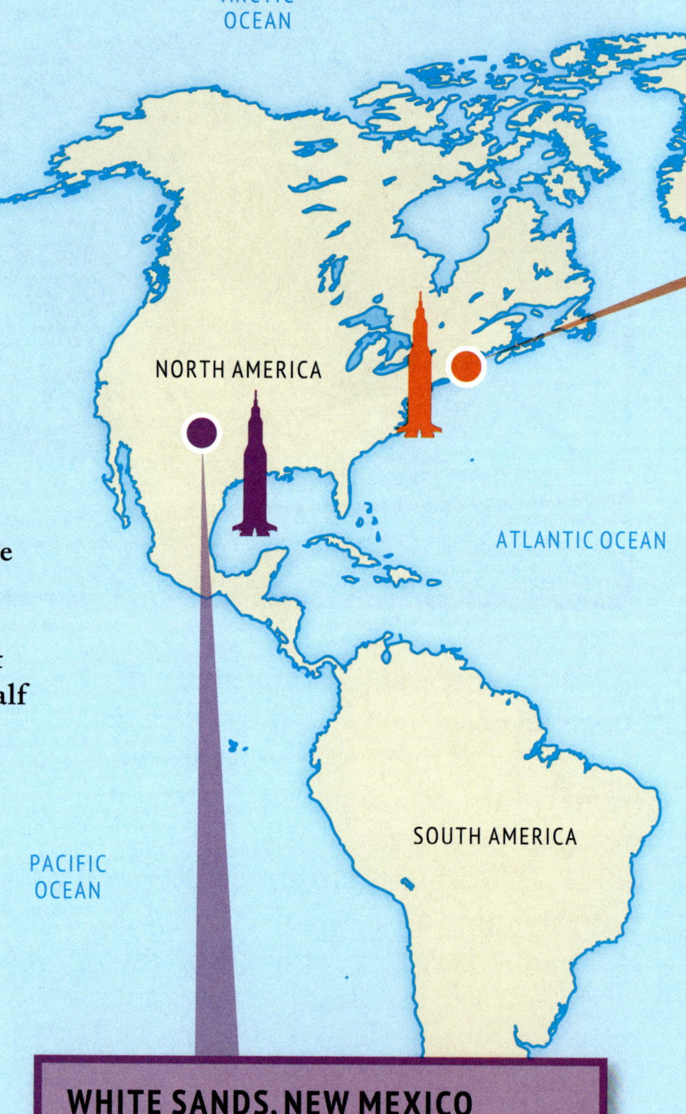

WHITE SANDS, NEW MEXICO

After World War II, several German scientists, including Wernher von Braun, worked for the United States at the White Sands Proving Grounds in New Mexico. Basing their initial work on captured V-2 missiles, they launched more than 60 rockets between 1946 and 1952. A smaller rocket on the nose of a V-2 produced the first two-stage rocket for high-altitude research.

AUBURN, MASSACHUSETTS

In 1926, American inventor Robert Goddard launched the first liquid-fuel rocket from his aunt's farm in Auburn and ushered in a new age. Fueled by gasoline and liquid oxygen, it reached a speed of 65 miles per hour (105 kilometers per hour) and climbed to a height of about 41 feet (12.5 m). By 1935, Goddard's rockets could reach more than 7,820 feet (2,400 m), at a speed of 620 miles per hour (1,000 kph).

ARCTIC OCEAN

ASIA

EUROPE

AFRICA

INDIAN OCEAN

AUSTRALIA

KALUGA, RUSSIA

Russian schoolteacher and astrophysicist Konstantin Tsiolkovsky formalized the modern theory of rocketry in 1903. He was the first person to suggest using rockets to reach space. He even proposed a liquid-fuel rocket powered by liquid hydrogen and liquid oxygen, the fuels used by most modern space rockets. Tsiolkovsky also invented the multistage rocket, which he called a "rocket train."

PEENEMÜNDE, GERMANY

By 1931, German scientist Hermann Oberth had developed a gasoline-liquid oxygen rocket. In 1930, a young engineering student, Wernher von Braun, joined Oberth's team. In 1936, the team was allocated a facility at Peenemünde on the Baltic Sea, where von Braun led research that produced the V-1 and the V-2. The V-1 was a pulsejet-powered flying bomb, while the V-2 was the first rocket-powered guided missile. The Germans used the weapons to bomb England late in World War II (1939–1945).

ACTIVITIES

Google Maps

Rockets

Examine the development of early rocketry centers around the world.

1. Why were the early rocket centers developed in these locations? What type of infrastructure was required for the development and research of rocketry?
2. How has space travel affected these sites? Have they been positively or negatively affected? In what ways?
3. What other countries might become important centers of rocketry and space research in the twenty-first century? Justify your conclusions.

Penicillin and Antibiotics

From the late nineteenth century, scientists and medical researchers recognized a new type of enemy. These were **bacteria**, or "germs." Many bacteria had been identified, and the diseases they caused were better understood. In the 1890s, Paul Ehrlich, a German bacteriologist, realized that it ought to be possible to kill germs invading the human body if the right drug for the task could be found. This was the so-called magic bullet theory. A specific chemical would be used to target a particular kind of cell or microorganism.

Ehrlich was particularly concerned with syphilis, a crippling disease. He searched for a synthetic chemical that could be injected into a patient to kill the bacterium that causes syphilis. After more than 600 chemicals were tested, Salvarsan appeared in 1910. It was the first synthetic magic bullet.

In the 1920s and 1930s, scientists sought other magic bullets that could be used against infectious diseases. Many chemicals proved harmful to human cells or did not work well. In the late 1930s, researchers developed a range of related drugs called sulfonamides, or sulfa drugs, that were effective against bacterial diseases. These drugs were at the forefront of disease treatment in the early 1940s.

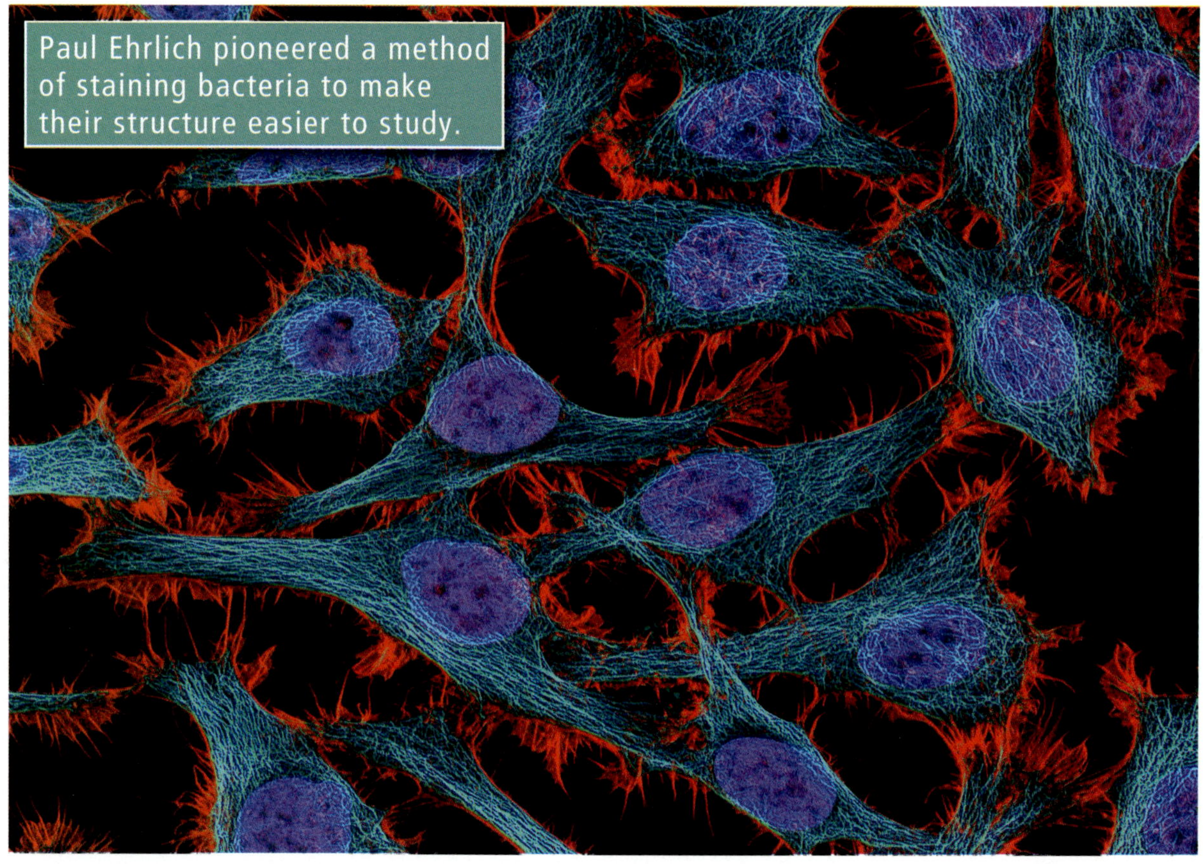

Paul Ehrlich pioneered a method of staining bacteria to make their structure easier to study.

An Amazing Discovery

The same kinds of organisms that caused disease also infected wounds. Wound infection was the specialty of Scottish bacteriologist Alexander Fleming. In 1921, he had made his name by discovering the **enzyme** lysozyme, produced by living cells to break down organic material. Fleming thought natural substances could hold the key to fighting bacterial infection. In 1928, he discovered penicillin, which could destroy a large range of bacteria.

Treatment Begins

Producing penicillin in large quantities was left to a team of scientists at Oxford University, England, led by Australian pathologist Howard Florey and biochemist Ernst Chain, a refugee from Nazi Germany. By 1940, they had extracted penicillin that enabled mice to fight off otherwise fatal infections. Tests with human patients were impressive enough to convince several pharmaceutical companies of penicillin's importance. Thanks to refinements in production developed by English biochemist Norman Heatley, the "miracle" drug was being mass-produced in the United States and Britain by about 1943. The development could not have come at a more crucial time. World War II (1939–1945) was raging, and wounded servicemen were the first to benefit. Toward the end of the war in Europe, in 1944, there were sufficient supplies of penicillin to treat all injured **Allied** soldiers who were in danger of infection.

Discovery of Penicillin

In 1928, after returning to his laboratory from vacation, Alexander Fleming noticed something unusual about a culture of Staphylococcus he had left in a petri dish. In his absence, a mold had grown in the dish. There were no colonies of bacteria around the mold, which also appeared to be killing the Staphylococcus. Through experiments, Fleming identified the mold as a species of Penicillium. He discovered that the liquid it produced, which he called penicillin, destroyed a large number of different bacteria. More exciting still, when tested on laboratory animals, it appeared to have no effect on healthy living tissue. The new treatment had drawbacks, however. It had no effect on several bacteria, notably those responsible for **plague** and cholera. Even more disheartening was the fact that penicillin turned out to be very difficult to produce. For every milliliter of fluid secreted from the Penicillium mold, only about 0.000002 milliliters was active penicillin, and what tiny amounts could be extracted deteriorated very easily.

Document

Alexander Fleming. Penicillin. Nobel Lecture, December 11, 1945

Analyze the key points of Fleming's Nobel lecture.

1. How does Fleming describe the beginning of penicillin? Why does he say that it was discovered not as a result of his previous work as a bacteriologist, but simply as an unwanted contamination of one of his culture plates? How was he able to recognize the importance of this mishap when it took place?
2. How is the first antibiotic that Fleming discovered in 1922 important in understanding penicillin? Why might an otherwise harmless drug cause death if used in insufficient quantities?

Weblink

The History of Antibiotics

Analyze the history and impact of antibiotics.

1. Why might antibiotics be considered to be one of the most significant medical achievements of the twentieth century? What impact have they had on the medical world and on the lives of everyday people?
2. What problems are now being faced worldwide due to antibiotic resistance? What can be done to combat antibiotic resistance?

Artificial Fibers

For centuries, weavers had only four fibers for making cloth. These were silk, wool, cotton, and flax, which was used to make linen. Weavers also used jute and hemp to produce coarse cord and sacking. The first attempts at creating an artificial fiber tried to copy the smooth, light feel of silk.

Natural silk consists of the plant product **cellulose**. Methods of copying it involve dissolving cellulose in the form of wood pulp or cotton to make a solution. The solution is forced through a tiny hole to make a strand. Chemicals harden the strand to form a fiber. The first patent for such a process was awarded in the early 1800s, to the Swiss chemist Georges Audemars. In 1883, English physicist Joseph Swan patented a process for making cellulose fibers by dissolving nitrocellulose in acetic acid, and forcing it through small holes.

In France in 1884, chemist Hilaire de Chardonnet tried to imitate the silk-making process. He made cotton waste into cellulose acetate, dissolved it in a solvent, and forced the solution through a mesh of small holes. The fiber became known as acetate rayon.

Viscose is used to make soft linings for clothing and garments such as shirts and skirts.

Chemists working in Germany produced a product called Glanzstoff. They dissolved cellulose in copper sulfate and ammonium hydroxide. In 1892, English chemists Edward Bevan and Charles Cross dissolved cellulose in sodium hydroxide and carbon disulfide. They forced the solution through a fine mesh and regenerated the cellulose by running the strands through a bath of sulfuric acid. This became known as the viscose process. The product was called viscose rayon.

Polymers

The first artificial fiber made without cellulose was produced in 1935, by U.S. chemist Wallace Carothers. It was a **polymer**. Carothers named his new product Nylon 66.

Carothers's company was DuPont. It first released the product in 1938. DuPont and other companies have produced several other kinds of nylon in the decades since.

In 1941, chemists John Whinfield and James Dickson created a different type of polymer. It was a polyester with the trade names Dacron and Terylene. This fiber is often blended with a natural fiber such as wool. More hardwearing than rayon and more resistant to heat than nylon, this polyester also holds color better than either of these products. In the 1950s, U.S. industrial chemists produced Orlon. Acrilan, another kind of acrylic fiber, dates from about the same time.

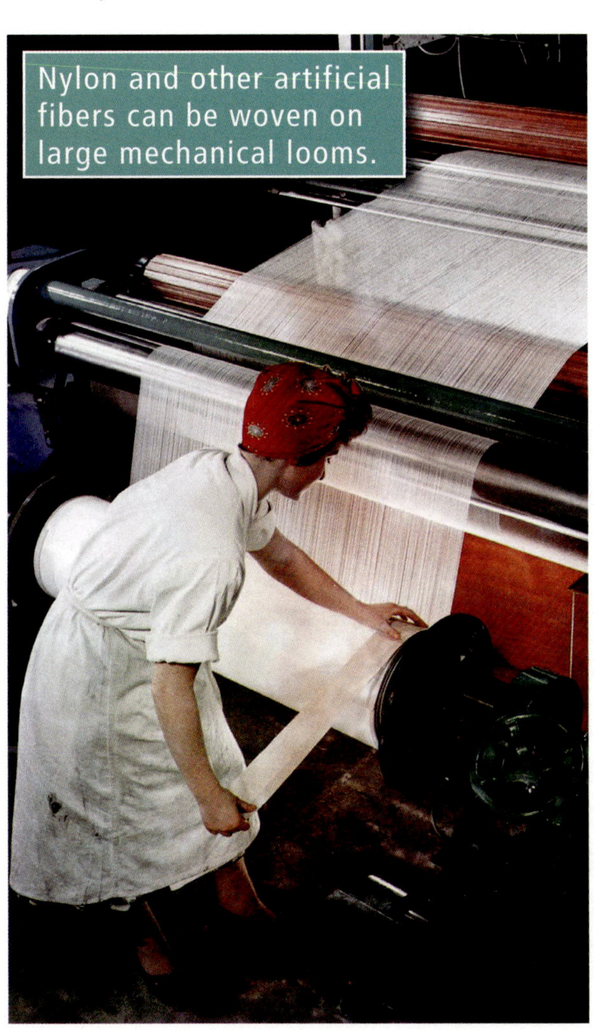
Nylon and other artificial fibers can be woven on large mechanical looms.

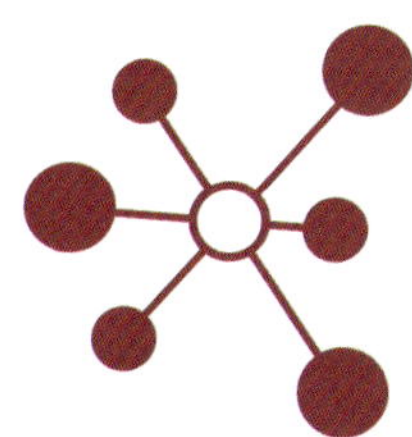

6
ATOMS
The number of carbon atoms in each of the starting chemicals, or monomers, used to create nylon 66

500
HOLES
The number of holes in a spinneret, the device used to extrude artificial fibers

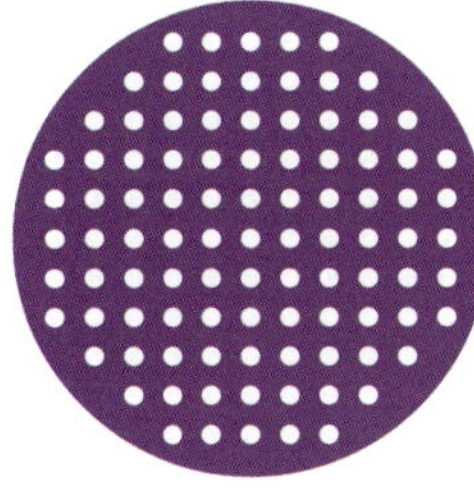

Other Products

Joseph Swan originally developed cellulose fibers for use as carbon filaments in electric lamps. In 1964, the U.S. company Hercules and the British company Courtaulds both reinvented carbon fibers. Carbon-fiber composites are made into items such as golf clubs, tennis rackets, and sailboat masts, as well as turbine blades and helicopter rotors.

Other inorganic substances used to make fibers include glass and asbestos. Glass fibers can be woven into cloth or used to reinforce carpets and materials for tents. They can be added to synthetic resins to make fiberglass, which has many applications, including boat hulls and car bodies. Cloth woven from asbestos is fireproof and can be used for gloves and protective clothing for firefighters.

ACTIVITIES

First Hand

Biographical Memoir : Wallace Carothers
Examine the life and work of Wallace Carothers.

1. Why did Carothers give up an academic career as professor of organic chemistry at Harvard in order to join a commercial company? What could Harvard have done to persuade Carothers to stay? How successful might these attempts have been?
2. How important was Carothers' work? What effect did his discoveries have on industry and society? Briefly summarize your conclusions.

Weblink

Fiber History
Analyze the development of artificial fibers and their impact on people around the world.

1. Why did people want to create artificial fibers when cotton, linen, wool, silk, and flax have been used for centuries? What are the advantages of using artificial fibers? What are the disadvantages?
2. Why did William Carothers name his polymers Nylon 66? Why was it thought to be a "miracle" fiber? Is this an accurate assessment for the time? Why or why not?
3. How are manufactured fibers used today? Do manufactured fibers continue to mean "life made better?" Why or why not?

RUBRIC

Analyzing a Scientific Biography

Students will research the life of a scientific figure and present their findings. An exemplary biographical analysis will meet the following criteria:

- Illustrates strong knowledge of the subject
- Identifies the author of the biography
- Describes why the subject of the biography is important
- Contains information about the time and place in which the subject was born
- Lists important events in the subject's life
- Explains how events in the subject's life impacted him or her
- Makes inferences about the subject based on events in his or her life
- Explains how the subject influenced the world while he or she lived
- Researches the cultural and historical context of the subject's life
- Examines the effect that the subject has had on the modern world
- Supplements information from the biography with independent research
- Organizes the analysis in a logical, effective manner
- Uses correct spelling, grammar, and punctuation
- Cites all sources used in the analysis

The Helicopter

As early as 1480, Italian artist and inventor Leonardo da Vinci sketched a design for an aircraft with a vertically mounted screw. He reasoned that if the screw rotated fast enough the craft would rise into the air. Four centuries later, in 1877, Italian physician Carlo Forlanini and Frenchman Gustave de Ponton d'Amécourt made model helicopters. Forlanini's model had a pair of **rotors** driven by a small steam engine. They lifted the craft to a height of 49 feet (15 meters), where it hovered.

By 1900, the gasoline engine was in use. In 1905, English engineer E.R. Mumford patented a machine with six 25-foot (7.5-m) propellers and a bamboo airframe. In 1912, the machine, tethered by ropes, lifted a pilot 10 feet (3 m) into the air. French brothers Jacques and Louis Bréguet also used a gasoline engine. In 1907, they built a machine with four rotors. Each blade resembled pairs of biplane wings, giving 32 rotor "blades" in all. With one of their assistants on board, the tethered Bréguet craft rose to a height of 24 inches (60 centimeters) for about a minute. Two months later, the first free flight in a helicopter was made by French bicycle engineer Paul Cornu. His longest flight lasted just 20 seconds, and he only lifted 6.5 feet (2 m) off the ground.

Human power alone could not have produced enough energy to raise Leonardo's flying machine off the ground, so it could never have flown.

Development Continues

Neither of the French machines successfully tackled the problem of directional stability, which is crucial for sustained flight. Between 1908 and 1912, Russian-born engineer Igor Sikorsky tried to solve the problem. He emigrated to the United States in 1919, where he continued to build experimental machines. The challenge was also taken up by others, including the U.S. electrical engineer Peter Cooper Hewitt, Louis Bréguet and René Dorand in France, and Heinrich Focke in Germany in 1936.

Keeping the Helicopter Stable

The helicopter has major aerodynamic problems. The first relates to the torque, or twisting effect, of the large rotor, which spins the fuselage in the opposite direction. Sikorsky devised a vertical tail rotor that pushes against the spin. The second problem is that the rotor blades are affected by the speed at which the helicopter is moving. In forward flight, the rotor blade moving against the airflow produces more lift than the blade moving with the airflow. The result makes an aircraft unstable. Hinges are attached to the blades to allow the blades to "flap" slightly to smooth the imbalance.

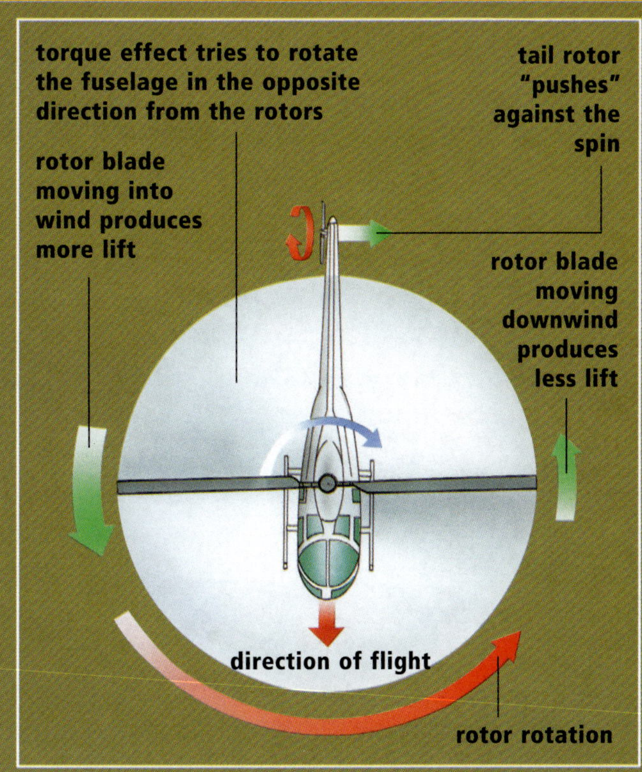

Focke's Fa-61 twin-rotor machine could fly backward as well as forward at a speed of 75 miles per hour (120 kilometers per hour), and a height of more than 7,800 feet (2,400 m). It set a sustained flight record of 1 hour 20 minutes. In 1938, German pilot Hanna Reitsch demonstrated the machine in Berlin.

Finally, in 1939, Sikorsky flew the first practical single-rotor machine. It could take off vertically, and reached a forward speed of 43 miles per hour (70 kph). It had an enclosed cabin, and a latticework tail carrying a small vertical propeller. This overcame the longstanding problem of **torque** in a single-rotor machine, since it kept the whole machine from rotating. During the early years of World War II (1939–1945), U.S. and British forces used versions of the Sikorsky VS-300 helicopter. The U.S. Army acquired its first machines in May 1942, and the British Royal Navy took delivery of the powerful Sikorsky R-4 in 1943.

The military helicopter came into its own during the Korean War (1950–1953). It transported troops and casualties. New helicopter gunships carried heavy cannon and acted as a form of aerial artillery. These were used extensively by U.S. forces in the Vietnam War (1959–1975).

ACTIVITIES

Transparency

What Is a Helicopter?

Examine the diagram showing the aerodynamics of a helicopter.

1. How was Sikorsky able to stabilize the flight? What other methods could be employed to attain the same results?
2. How does a helicopter's curved-edge rotor blades contribute to lift? How does less pressure under the rotor blade create lift?

Weblink

Igor Sikorsky: Aviation Pioneer

Evaluate Igor Sikorsky's contributions to aviation.

1. What was Sikorsky internationally famous for before moving to the United States? Why did he immigrate in 1919?
2. Why did the composer Sergei Rachmaninoff help Sikorsky to fund his first aviation business?
3. When did Sikorsky first become interested in single rotor vertical flight aircraft? Why did he have to wait nearly 30 years before seeing his vision make its first flight?

Development of Radar

Radar stands for "radio detecting and ranging." To detect an object, a radar transmits a pulse of high-frequency **radio waves**, and a receiving antenna picks up any echoes that return. The returning signal reveals the direction and range of any object it bounces off.

In 1904, German engineer Christian Hülsmeyer took out the first patents for such a device. He planned a system to warn ships of possible collisions at sea. In 1922, engineers at the U.S. Naval Research Laboratory detected passing ships when they interrupted a radio beam. In Britain, Scottish physicist Robert Watson-Watt was asked by the Admiralty to investigate the use of radio beams, and found that he could detect aircraft. Using the British Broadcasting Corporation's powerful transmitter, he detected a bomber flying 7.5 miles (12 km) away at a height of 9,800 feet (3,000 m). He patented his system in 1935. With World War II approaching, the British built a chain of radar antennas on tall towers along the eastern and southern coastline of England. They detected incoming airplanes at a range of up to 200 miles (320 km) away.

Allied engineers set up portable radar stations as they advanced in Europe and North Africa.

By the end of World War II, Britain's coast was guarded by more than 40 radar stations.

invented by Henri Gutton. The cavity magnetron used a resonant "chamber," or cavity, to create the signals. Two researchers at Birmingham University, John Randall and Henry Boot, developed the device in 1939. The equipment generated **wavelengths** as small as 3.5 inches (9 cm), and a radar using it could detect a submarine periscope 7 miles (11 km) away. The British immediately gave details of the cavity magnetron to researchers in the United States. An alternative radar tube, the klystron, was invented in 1938, by U.S. radio engineers Russell and Sigurd Varian.

Gun-aiming Radar

Engineers also adapted radars to aim guns, particularly antiaircraft and long-range naval guns. Rudolf Kühnold was Germany's radar pioneer. In 1933, he demonstrated a prototype to the navy. By 1936, several German warships had been fitted with gunnery radar. In the United States, Canadian-born engineer Lawrence Hyland renewed official interest in antiaircraft and aircraft-detection radars. He demonstrated a system on the USS *New York* in 1939.

The Magnetron

The very high frequencies of radar signals require special electronics. Early transmitters used a **vacuum tube** called a magnetron, invented by U.S. physicist Albert Hull in 1921. An improved version came in about 1934, from the French company CSF,

Radar in Peacetime

After World War II, radar found more and more peacetime applications. In 1946, astronomers picked up radar signals reflected back from the Moon, and, in 1958, echoes came back from the planet Venus. Soviet astronomers made radar contact with Mercury in 1962, and Mars in 1963. The National Aeronautics and Space Administration (NASA) has used orbiting space probes to map the beds of Earth's oceans and the surface of Venus. Weather forecasters rely on satellite radar, archaeologists use radar to search for buried ruins, and law enforcement agencies employ it to detect speeding motorists.

ACTIVITIES

Video

Introduction to Radar
Analyze the role of radar in aviation history.

1. Why was radar so important during the Battle of Britain? How would the battle have been different without it? Would it have changed the conclusion? Why or why not?
2. What prompted the setting up of air traffic control systems for commercial usage in the post-war years? What systems are used by air traffic control centers today? How have they been improved over time?

Weblink

The Development of Radar
Examine the development of radar and the principles behind it.

1. What are the basic principles of radar systems? Why was the magnetron so important to the effective development of radar? Is the claim that the superiority of the Allies' radar systems resulted in victory in World War II valid? Explain your conclusions.
2. What part did the threat of war play in the research and development of radar? Why was the Chain Home radar network set up in Britain shortly before World War II?

RUBRIC

Answering a Scientific Question

Research the pros and cons of producing electricity with nuclear energy. Write a report on your investigation. An exemplary report will meet the following criteria:

- The problem is written in the form of a question with a question mark at the end
- The hypothesis is written as a guess or explanation to the answer of the problem
- The hypothesis is written in a complete sentence. (I think ..., I hypothesize ..., If.. then...)
- The variable and controls are clearly identified
- Procedure steps are in numbered order
- Procedure steps show what to measure and where to record the data
- Procedure steps are written in complete sentences
- The data is organized in a data table
- The experiment or investigation includes more then one trial
- All numbers have labels (cm., ml., g.)
- All calculations complete
- Conclusion written in complete sentences
- Conclusion states whether your hypothesis was right or wrong
- Conclusion answers the question written in the problem

The first working nuclear reactor used rods of uranium and 45,000 graphite blocks.

Nuclear Fission

In 1932, English physicist John Cockcroft and Irish physicist Ernest Walton began experimenting with high-energy protons in their particle accelerator in Cambridge, England. In Paris in 1934, French physicists Irène and Frédéric Joliot-Curie found that proton bombardment sometimes produced **radioactive isotopes** of the target atoms. Two years later, Italian-American physicist Enrico Fermi found that neutrons, which had been discovered in 1932 by English physicist James Chadwick, were more effective than protons at smashing atoms.

Neutron bombardment usually produced heavier atoms through neutron absorption. When Fermi bombarded atoms of heavy elements, especially uranium, he found that much lighter nuclei were produced. In 1938, German physicists Otto Hahn and Fritz Strassmann identified the products of the bombardment as elements with about half the mass of uranium. The uranium nuclei had broken apart. Fission had occurred. The same year, Lise Meitner, an Austrian-born physicist, and her Austrian nephew Otto Frisch, working in Copenhagen with Danish physicist Niels Bohr, explained this result. The uranium nucleus absorbed a neutron, causing it to vibrate violently.

The neutron divided into two parts, releasing energy. Fission also released neutrons that could trigger fission in other nuclei. This meant that a chain reaction could release a huge amount of energy in a weapon. In a nuclear reactor, a sustainable chain reaction could also generate energy that could be harnessed and used as electricity.

A Chain Reaction

Three isotopes of uranium occur naturally. Bohr calculated that fission would occur more readily in rare Uranium-235U, so a way was found to separate the isotopes, a technique known as "enrichment." Bohr also realized that fission would be more effective if the neutrons were slowed down. Fermi and Hungarian-born physicist Leo Szilard suggested surrounding the uranium with a "moderator," such as graphite or **heavy water** that slows neutrons.

The atomic chain reaction uses fission to split uranium-235 into more 235U and 236U.

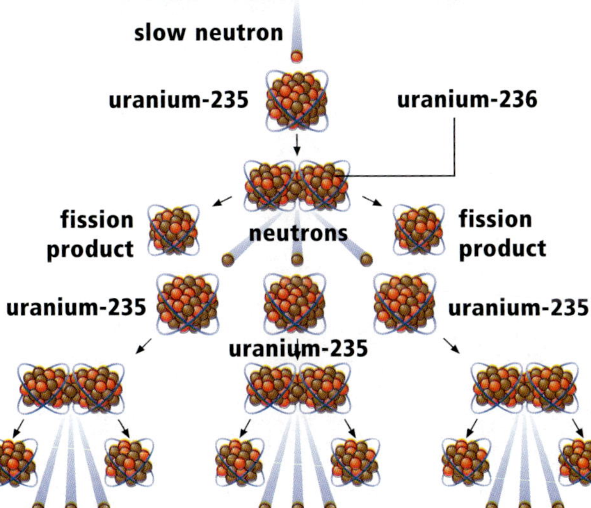

Using Nuclear Energy

Two days before the outbreak of World War II in 1939, Niels Bohr and U.S. theoretical physicist John Wheeler published a paper describing the complete fission process. Also in 1939, French physicist Francis Perrin showed that a "critical mass" of uranium is needed to sustain a chain reaction by ensuring that enough of the neutrons released strike other uranium nuclei. Rudolf Peierls, a German-born physicist working in England, developed these ideas. Designed by Enrico Fermi (above) and called "an atomic pile," the first self-sustaining working reactor began operating on December 2, 1942, at the University of Chicago. In 1951, the Experimental Breeder Reactor, built at Idaho National Engineering Laboratory near Idaho Falls, Idaho, became the first reactor in the world to generate electricity.

ACTIVITIES

Document

Historic Milestone: Nuclear News, November 2001

Examine the report written on the 50th anniversary of Idaho's Experimental Breeder Reactor, EBR–1.

1. What was the stated aim of the scientists behind the EBR–1? Why were the celebrations subdued when the first light bulbs lit by nuclear energy went on at the breeder?
2. Why was the reactor closed down after operating for 12 years? What had scientists learned during its life?
3. How much electricity is produced by nuclear power in the United States today? Which alternate energy sources could be used to produce the same amount of power?

Weblink

Nuclear Fission

Analyze the difference between nuclear fission and nuclear fusion.

1. How does nuclear fission differ from nuclear fusion? Why does uranium make a good basis for nuclear fission?
2. Why were nuclear scientists able to make accurate predictions about the power of nuclear fission in the 1930s and early 1940s? How can the total energy released in fission be calculated?

First Computers

A computer is an electronic machine that performs tasks under instructions from a program. Digital computers handle data in the form of digits expressed in binary notation, which uses only two digits, 1 and 0, equivalent to on and off pulses of electric current. The first computers were used by the U.S. Army and Navy near the end of World War II. They were massive vacuum-tube machines, developed from electronic calculating machines of the late 1930s.

French scientist Blaise Pascal probably invented the first mechanical adding machine in 1642. It had a system of intermeshed cogs, a method adopted by English mathematician Charles Babbage in his "analytical engine" of 1833. Babbage's machine could be programmed for a particular calculation. Calculating machines with keyboards were developed from the 1880s.

Most early methods of feeding data into programmable machines used punched tape or punched cards. In about 1805, French inventor Joseph Jacquard designed a new loom. It could weave various patterns in carpets by following instructions on an endless belt of punched cards. American inventor Herman Hollerith employed similar cards to analyze the results of the 1890 U.S. census. He formed a company that later became part of International Business Machines (IBM). It still operates today.

A group of six women were responsible for programming ENIAC by moving its switches and cables, a process that could take days.

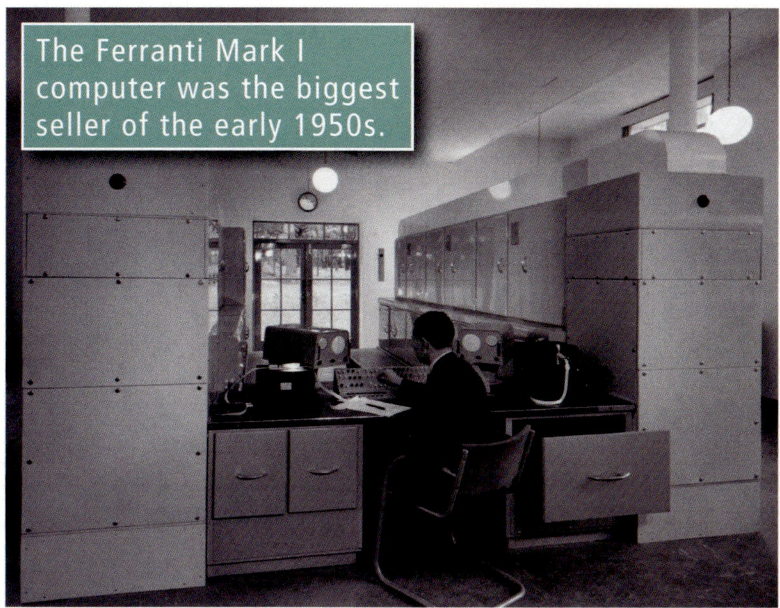
The Ferranti Mark I computer was the biggest seller of the early 1950s.

quantity in the United States. Eckert and Mauchly modified it to use **magnetic tape** storage. In 1949, a team at Manchester University, England, built a stored-program machine under the guidance of mathematician Alan Turing. The machine was so successful the British government asked the Ferranti company to manufacture it.

Coming of Electronics

Electromechanical calculators appeared in the 1930s. By 1942, John Atanasoff had built an electronic calculator called the ABC. Using vacuum tubes, it could also be programmed to process data, making it arguably the first true computer. Two years later, Harvard mathematician Howard Aiken devised a manually operated digital machine controlled by punched paper tape. In 1946, the all-electronic Electronic Numerical Integrator and Calculator (ENIAC) computer was brought into service, although it also employed vacuum tubes.

A machine built at Princeton in 1946 by American mathematician John von Neumann was the first with a stored program that used binary numbers. The idea was incorporated into UNIVAC I, designed by U.S. computer engineers John Eckert and John Mauchly in 1951. UNIVAC 1 was the first computer to be manufactured in

Integrated Circuits

After the invention of the transistor in the late 1940s, computers became faster and smaller. By the mid-1960s, silicon chips allowed circuits to incorporate microprocessors on single chips. Today, microchips are used not only in personal computers (PCs), tablets, and smartphones, but also in domestic appliances, automobiles, and industrial robots.

8
COMPUTERS
The number of Mark 1 computers made and sold by Ferranti in the early 1950s

3
TERMINALS
The minimum number of terminals possessed by a transistor to connect to electrical circuits

ACTIVITIES

Video

ENIAC: First Military Giant Brain Computer
Assess the accomplishments of ENIAC and its impact on future developments.

1. How valid is the claim that the computer carried out more calculation during its 10 years in service than all of humanity up to that point? How does the type of data it was processing impact this claim?
2. What other large-scale electronic computers were developed by the designers of ENIAC? What they were used for?

Weblink

Timeline of Computer History
Examine the history of computers and their impact on society.

1. In 1941, Konrad Zuse designed the Z3 to perform aerodynamic calculations. Why that would have been of particular importance at the time? Why was the existence of "Colossus" not made public until the 1970s?
2. Which advances in computer technology had the most impact on the development of the personal computer? How did they contribute to the personal computer's development?

RUBRIC

Analyzing a Primary Source

Students will complete a thorough analysis of a primary source on breaking the sound barrier. An exemplary analysis will meet the following criteria:

- Identifies the creator of the source
- Explains what medium was used to create the primary source
- Describes why the source qualifies as a primary one
- Explores any literary devices used in the source
- Identifies the intended audience for the source
- Relates the creator's goals in creating the source
- Illustrates knowledge of the period and location in which the source was created
- Distinguishes between facts and opinions found in the source
- Examines the reliability of the source's creator
- Compares the source with similar documents
- Cites additional sources used in the analysis
- Presents information in a clear, concise manner
- Uses correct spelling, grammar, and punctuation

Frank Whittle found it difficult to raise funding to develop a jet engine because the British government was not interested in the new idea.

Jet Aircraft

Air flowing over the surfaces of a propeller-driven airplane behaves like a fluid, generating lift. Some engineers realized that at speeds approaching 700 miles per hour (1,100 kph), the air behaves differently. Drag, or air resistance, increases to the point at which the air begins to form shock waves. As the airplane is buffeted by shock waves, it loses lift, and the pilot begins to lose control. The behavior of the air around a propeller limits the speeds that can be attained by aircraft. A new type of engine was needed if higher speeds were to be reached.

The Jet Engine

The military's need for faster aircraft encouraged the development of new engines. In the 1930s, scientists in both the United States and Germany were investigating the possibility of using rockets as airplane engines. The Germans were led by Wernher von Braun and the Americans by Robert Goddard. However, rocket engines proved to be too expensive and too explosive for practical use.

Meanwhile, in Britain, engineer Frank Whittle patented the jet engine in 1930. With some friends, he formed a company called Power Jets, Ltd. By 1937, Whittle and his associates had built an operational jet engine.

It was not until the 1950s, however, that the jet engine came into common use. There were many variations on Whittle's design. One of the first was the inclusion of an afterburner. By injecting more fuel into the hot exhaust gases after they had passed through the turbine, it was possible to increase the thrust produced by up to 40 percent. Another variation was the turbofan, which is a jet engine fitted with a large fan that drives air into the compressor and around the engine to give additional thrust.

Jet-powered Airplanes

The German company Heinkel built the first jet-powered aircraft. Engineers Hans von Ohain, Herbert Wagner, and Helmut Schelp worked on the jet engine independently of Whittle. On August 27, 1939, the Heinkel-built He-178 made its first flight. It took the outbreak of World War II to get the British government to take Whittle's ideas seriously, giving the Germans a head start. The Gloster Meteor, the Royal Air Force's first jet fighter, entered the war in 1944. By the end of World War II, it was clear to all sides that future combat planes would have to be jet-powered.

The Sound Barrier

Breaking the sound barrier became the goal of engineers at the U.S. Bell Aircraft Company. When Bell requested a test pilot for its secret new project, the X-1, U.S. Army fighter pilot Captain Charles "Chuck" Yeager volunteered. The X-1 was essentially a small rocket equipped with four combustion chambers fired independently. It had to be carried into the air beneath a Boeing B-29 bomber. At about 30,000 feet (9,100 m), the X-1 would drop from the B-2, and Yeager would fire the first of the rocket chambers.

On October 14, 1947, Yeager punched in the rocket engines of the X-1 over Rogers Dry Lake, southern California. He became the first person ever to fly faster than the speed of sound. At 43,000 feet (13,100 m), Yeager flew through the sound barrier at a speed of 700 miles per hour (1,127 kph).

The X-1 caused a bang called a sonic boom as it passed through the sound barrier.

ACTIVITIES

Video

Chuck Yeager Breaks the Sound Barrier

Assess the impact of Chuck Yeager breaking the sound barrier.

1. How was the speed of the X–1 monitored? Why was this the only way to time it accurately?
2. What advances were able to take place as a result of Chuck Yeager's actions? How might the world be different if this event had not taken place?

Weblink

The Birth of the Jet: The Engine that Shrunk the World

Analyze the process that resulted in the development of the jet engine.

1. What was Whittle's concept for improving flight speed and fuel efficiency? How did he arrive at this concept? Why was Whittle forced to form his own company in order to pursue his ideas?
2. Why was Hans von Ohain's HeS1 hydrogen engine revised to run on gasoline? How does Whittle's patented centrifugal-flow engine compare to Ohain's original centrifugal-flow design? Describe the similarities and differences.

RUBRIC

Developing a Scientific Argument

Research the controversial topic of genetically modified (GM) organisms online and present a scientific argument that explains your stance on the issue. An exemplary scientific argument will meet the following criteria.

- Provides background on the topic within the introduction
- Has a logical introduction and provides accurate scientific information
- Explains alternative opinions that are related to the controversy of the topic
- Explains the research, including critiques of websites
- Contains accurate scientific information. All relevant pieces of evidence are analyzed.
- Well-supported stance is justified by analysis
- Explanation of stance incorporates and explains personal opinions, as well as reflects on opinions that changed throughout the research process
- Usefulness and credibility of websites is discussed
- More than four websites are consulted, and sources are properly cited
- Free of grammatical and spelling errors

The Double Helix

In 1951, American chemist Linus Pauling developed a technique for resolving the structures of large biological molecules. He described a class of proteins where the molecules took the form of a helix, a three-dimensional spiral. He then focused on dioxyribonucleic acid (DNA), which scientists knew was a key part of chromosomes, the vital units of inheritance.

For biology graduate Francis Crick at Cambridge University, England, the structure of DNA was an obsession. Crick found a collaborator in James Watson, an American biophysicist who arrived at Cambridge in 1951. Watson and Crick began working on the problem. They were competing with a team at Kings College, London, that was already trying to decipher the structure of DNA.

Understanding DNA

In London, New Zealand-born British biophysicist Maurice Wilkins and English physical chemist Rosalind Franklin used **X-ray diffraction** to find the structure of DNA. Franklin had all but dismissed the idea that DNA might be a helix, but Watson and Crick thought otherwise. In 1951, they produced a model of DNA as a triple helix. Franklin was among the first to disagree. The structure did not conform to her data. Watson and Crick went back to the drawing board. In 1952, Linus Pauling presented his own model. This, too, showed the molecule as a helix with three intertwined strands.

DNA has four chemical compounds known as bases. The realization that these molecules pair off in a predictable way set Watson and Crick on the right track. They learned from the work of the Austrian-born chemist Erwin Chargaff, that the base adenine always paired with thymine, and that guanine paired with cytosine.

Rosalind Franklin figured out the molecular structure of crystals by scattering X-rays through them.

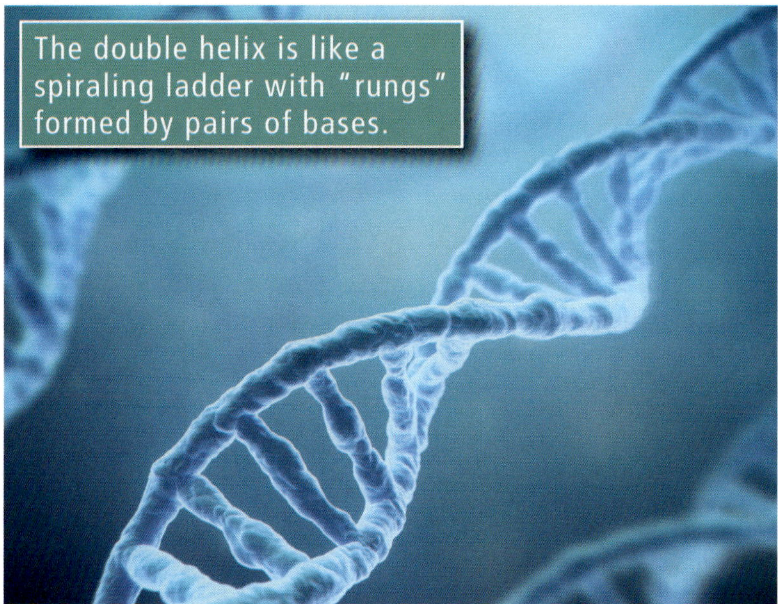
The double helix is like a spiraling ladder with "rungs" formed by pairs of bases.

Watson and Crick now understood not only the structure of DNA but how it replicates. They published their results in April 1953. In 1962, they won the Nobel Prize in Physiology or Medicine, together with Maurice Wilkins. Franklin had died in 1958, so was not considered for the prize.

DNA Tools

The late 1940s and early 1950s saw a number of scientists studying bacterial plasmids. Plasmids are tiny circlets of DNA that drift within the bacterial cytoplasm, separate from the main chromosome. They are easily isolated, modified, and reinserted into cells, so plasmids became one of the most important tools in modern genetics.

In Geneva in 1968, American Stuart Linn and Swiss biophysicist Werner Arber discovered a class of proteins called restriction enzymes that "cut" DNA in specific places. The cut ends readily bind back together or splice with the ends of other sections of DNA. In 1969, American geneticist Jonathan Beckwith succeeded in isolating a single gene involved in the metabolism of sugar in the bacterium *Escherichia coli*. Such steps made it theoretically possible to delete genes or to insert new ones into a sequence of DNA. In 1973, American biologists Stanley Cohen and Herbert Boyer removed a section of DNA from an *E. coli* plasmid and replaced it with a gene from a different bacterium. The result was the first genetically engineered organism. A new, exciting, and contentious branch of science was underway.

Genetic Engineering

Genetic engineering allows scientists to replace undesirable genes in an organism with desirable ones from another. The gene for human insulin was inserted into *E.coli*, and then into a yeast, in the 1980s, revolutionizing the production of a vital therapy for diabetics worldwide. In agriculture, similar processes are used to produce hardier, more productive crops. Debate continues over the widespread use of these techniques, and in some parts of the world there is mistrust of genetically modified (GM) organisms. Gene replacement therapies also promise to provide treatment for many genetically linked disorders.

ACTIVITIES

Document

Watson and Crick's Structure for Deoxyribose Nucleic Acid, Nature, April 25, 1953

Assess Watson and Crick's contributions to scientific understanding of DNA.

1. Why did Watson and Crick find Pauling and Corey's suggested structure for nucleic acid to be unsatisfactory? What was the most important thing that Watson and Crick discovered about DNA?
2. Why was Rosalind Franklin's contribution limited to a brief name check at the end of the article? Is this a fair reflection of her contribution? Why or why not?

Weblink

The Discovery of the Molecular Structure of DNA—THE DOUBLE HELIX

Evaluate the process by which DNA was discovered.

1. How did Gregor Mendel's experiments with peas connect with the discovery of DNA? What were his conclusions?
2. How did Oswald Avery prove the connection between genes and nucleic acid? Why did this lead scientists to believe the DNA was likely the molecule of life? Summarize the conclusion.

The cyclotron was one of the first particle accelerators used to search for new elements.

New Chemical Elements

Until 1937, there were four gaps in the Periodic Table up to element number 92, which is uranium. The gaps were at elements 43, 61, 85, and 87. In 1937, scientists in California used the cyclotron to bombard the metal molybdenum with deuterons, which are nuclei of deuterium. They sent a sample of the bombarded molybdenum to physicists Emilio Segrè and Carlo Perrier at Palermo University in Italy. The Italians found the sample contained a new radioactive element, the missing number 43. They named it masurium, but later renamed it technetium.

In 1939, French chemist Marguerite Perey examined radioactive decay in actinium-227, and discovered another new radioactive element, the missing number 87. She originally called it actinium-K, but later changed the name to francium in honor of her native land.

Segrè and his coworkers went on to discover element 85 in 1940, when they bombarded bismuth with alpha particles, which are helium nuclei. The new element was nonradioactive. In 1947, they named the element astatine. Other scientists later discovered heavier isotopes of astatine. It is the rarest naturally occurring element on Earth.

The final missing element from the Periodic Table was element 61. It was found in 1945, when U.S. chemist Jacob Marinsky bombarded neodymium with neutrons. He named the element promethium. Prometheus stole fire from the gods in Greek myth.

Making New Elements

Particle bombardment can build up new particles. In 1940, U.S. chemists Edwin McMillan and Philip Abelson bombarded uranium-238 with neutrons to make neptunium, named for Neptune. A team led by McMillan and Glenn Seaborg then bombarded uranium-238 with deuterium nuclei. They created plutonium, named for the dwarf planet Pluto, which orbits beyond Neptune.

Element 109 was named meitnerium for Austrian-Swedish physicist Lise Meitner, one of the first scientists to split the atom.

61
EMPTY SPACE
The last gap on the Periodic Table to be filled, with promethium, in 1945.

118
ELEMENTS
The total number of elements on the Periodic Table accepted by most scientists in the 2010s.

Neptunium and plutonium were the first transuranic elements, or elements with an atomic number greater than that of uranium. Others followed, including curium (1944), americium (1944), berkelium (1949), and californium (1950), and seaborgium (1974). In 1982, German physicist Peter Armbruster made a few atoms of element 109 by bombarding bismuth-209 with nuclei of iron-58. In 1984, the same team produced some atoms of element 108, hassium, by bombarding lead-208 with nuclei of iron-58. Russian scientists also produced hassium by the same method, and in 1985, a Russian-American team made a different isotope of element 108 by bombarding uranium-238 with sulfur-34. There are now more than 115 chemical elements, although the precise number is disputed. Even heavier elements are possible in theory, but anything heavier than element 120 would be so unstable that it could have only a fleeting existence.

ACTIVITIES

Document

Glenn Seaborg's Nobel Lecture 1951: The Transuranium Elements: Present Status

Evaluate the work of Glenn Seaborg after reading his Nobel lecture.

1. How does a cyclotron work? What were the "deuterons" that Seaborg used? What role did they play in the cyclotron's operation?
2. Can modern scientific developments take place without a team of researchers? Why or why not?

Weblink

How Many More Chemical Elements Are There For Us to Find?

Assess the steps being taken to discover new elements.

1. Why is an eighth row of the periodic table an exciting prospect for scientists? What effects could an eighth shell of electrons have on an element?
2. Why did Richard Feynman believe that an atom with 137 protons could not exist? Why was his calculation not correct?

RUBRIC

Analyzing a Scientific Video

Students will watch and assess a video related to a scientific discovery or event, and write an analysis of the video. An exemplary video analysis will meet the following criteria:

- Identifies the purpose of the video
- Identifies the intended audience of the video
- Identifies the video as a primary or secondary source
- Discusses the scientific and social context of the video
- Describes how the content of the video is presented
- Summarizes the information and opinions presented in the video
- Analyzes the quality of the content presented in the video
- Assesses the effectiveness of the video
- Determines whether the images and graphics used in the video relate to the content
- Determines whether the video is easy to follow and understand
- Gives the analysis a clear and consistent purpose
- Organizes the analysis in a logical, effective manner
- Presents a strong, clear argument about the video
- Provides strong and accurate details to support the argument about the video
- Considers other perspectives on the purpose and effectiveness of the video
- Cites all sources used in the analysis

Radio Telescopes

The American radio engineer Karl Jansky detected radio waves from outer space in 1931, using an improvised antenna. Six years later, another American engineer, Grote Reber, built a steerable radio telescope and began to search the heavens for radio signals. The telescope had a dish-shaped antenna 31 feet (9.4 m) across, and received signals at a wavelength of 1.9 meters. Radio wavelengths are longer than those of light, so radio telescopes have to be much larger than the mirrors of reflecting telescopes to achieve similar resolution. By 1942, Reber had used a wavelength of 23.6 inches (60 cm) to build a radio map of the Universe.

In 1946, British scientists studying the Cygnus constellation located a strong fluctuating radio source. They named it Cygnus A. By this time, astronomers had access to microwave radio equipment developed for radar during World War II (1939–1945), but more powerful telescopes were needed to study radio galaxies.

In 1948, English astronomer Martin Ryle built a radio interferometer. The device used two widely separated radio telescopes. Ryle used it to detect hundreds of radio sources in outer space, including Cygnus A. These radio sources were all carefully cataloged and published. Ryle went on to build larger interferometers, including, in 1955, a version that had four separate antennas.

Jodrell Bank was built to observe cosmic rays.

Single Telescopes

The first large single radio telescope was constructed in England in 1957, under the supervision of radio astronomer Bernard Lovell. Jodrell Bank's 250-foot (76.2-m) radio dish achieved fame almost immediately when it tracked Earth's first artificial satellite, the Soviet Sputnik 1. Other, large steerable telescopes followed, including the Parkes Radio Telescope, at 209 feet (64 m) across, in Australia, completed in 1961, and the 328-foot (100-m) dishes at Effelsberg in Germany, and Green Bank in Virginia. Cornell University completed the largest telescope of its type over a natural depression in the ground at Arecibo in northwestern Puerto Rico. It consists of an aluminum mesh 1,000 feet (305 m) across, with a radio receiver hanging on wires at its focus. The telescope was built in 1963 and upgraded in 1974 and 1997.

Each radio telescope in the Very Large Array in New Mexico is 82 feet (25 m) wide.

Probing the Universe

Even such huge dishes can only detect limited detail at long distances. To obtain greater detail, astronomers returned to the principle of the interferometer. They came up with a system of using two or more radio telescopes together. The telescopes are mounted on railroad tracks to easily vary the distances between them. Communications cables carry signals from the telescopes to a computer, which uses the tiny differences between signals to resolve as much detail as possible. The computer also controls the aiming of the telescopes, which is critical in bad weather.

Radio astronomers use this technique to employ separate telescopes in the technique known as a Very Large Array (VLA). In 1980, the National Radio Astronomy Observatory completed a VLA in New Mexico, which has 27 antennas on a Y-shaped track extending 19 miles (32 km). It is as powerful as a single dish 22 miles (36 km) across. The very long baseline array (VLBA) was completed in 1993. It includes 10 radio telescopes in the United States and its territories from the Virgin Islands to Hawaii. In this way, Reber's original antenna has become a radio telescope equivalent to a dish thousands of miles across, capable of reaching into the farthest recesses of the Universe.

ACTIVITIES

Video

Jodrell Bank: 100 Hours of Astronomy

Assess the importance of the Jodrell Bank Observatory.

1. Why did Bernard Lovell initially set up the Lovell radio telescope at Jodrell Bank Observatory? What were the benefits of choosing this location? What were the drawbacks?
2. How has the observatory impacted scientists' understanding of the skies? What might not have been discovered if the observatory had not existed?

Weblink

What Is Radio Astronomy?

Analyze the contributions that radio astronomy has made to science.

1. What are the basic differences between optical telescopes and radio telescopes? Why is the resolution of optical telescopes superior?
2. What size would the dish of a single radio telescope need to be to have the same resolution as an optical telescope? Why would this be impractical? How has interferometry solved the problem of resolution?

RUBRIC

Writing an Abstract

Students will use their library to find a scientific research article or study related to Theodore Maiman and laser technology, then write a 300-word abstract. An exemplary abstract will meet the following criteria:

- States the research question or problem that the author is answering
- Indicates the significance of the issue
- Describes and explains methods used by the scientist(s)
- Explains why the methods used by the scientist(s) were appropriate
- Explains why this article or study stands out and how it is different from others
- Clearly states how the article or study advances knowledge about the topic, why it is important, and how it can be used
- Provides an introductory statement that is clear, concise, and engaging
- Has a clear, concise, and relevant purpose
- Provides explanations of findings including what was expected, discovered, accomplished, collected, and produced
- Clearly states the conclusion
- Describes how the work contributes to the field
- Writing is appropriate and free from grammatical errors

Lasers

A laser beam can cut metal more precisely than a saw. Lasers are also used in delicate eye surgery. Surveyors use lasers to measure distances, and lasers mounted on aircraft produce the detail needed to make highly accurate maps of the ground surface. Some computer printers use laser technology as well.

In 1917, German-born physicist Albert Einstein recognized the principle behind the laser. He argued that it should be possible to stimulate atoms and molecules to emit light. It was not until the 1950s, however, that physicists described a device that could generate a laser beam. In 1952, U.S. physicist Charles H. Townes described a way to stimulate molecules of ammonia to emit microwaves using the principle of the maser, which stands for microwave amplification by stimulated emission of radiation. Two Soviet physicists, Aleksandr Prokhorov and Nikolai Basov, had the same idea. However, by the time they came to publish it, Townes had built the first maser in 1953. The three scientists received the 1964 Nobel Prize in Physics for their discovery. Today, masers are used in atomic clocks and radio telescopes, and to amplify weak signals from satellites.

Principle of the Laser

Microwave radiation is invisible, but in 1958, Townes and Arthur Schawlow, another American physicist, published a paper showing that it was theoretically possible to make a device that would emit visible light. This device produced light amplification by stimulated emission of radiation, giving it the name laser. Townes and Schawlow did not go on to construct such a device, however. Instead, it was American physicist Theodore H. Maiman who made the first laser in 1960.

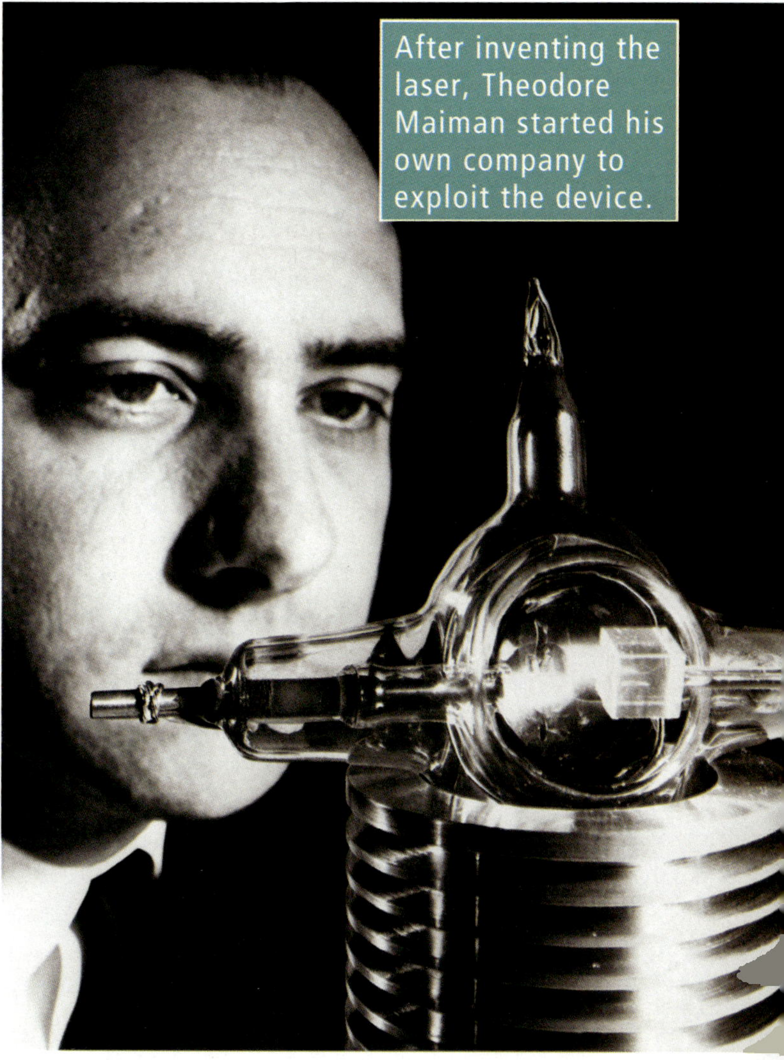

After inventing the laser, Theodore Maiman started his own company to exploit the device.

Modern laser tools used in manufacturing can be precisely made using 3D printing.

When a substance absorbs energy such as heat, its atoms or molecules jump from a low-energy level to a high-energy level. As they drop back to the low-energy level, they emit surplus energy in the form of light. Ordinarily, each of the atoms or molecules emits light independently of the others and at different wavelengths. If the substance is exposed to very intense light of a particular wavelength during the brief instant it is at its high-energy level, however, it will emit light at the same wavelength as the light shining on it. That stimulates the substance, which further intensifies the light.

The next step is to amplify the light by the use of mirrors. A mirror at one end of the device reflects light back through the substance that is being stimulated. A half-silvered mirror at the opposite end reflects some of the light, but lets the remainder escape as a laser beam.

Beam of Light

A laser emits a narrow beam of coherent light of a single wavelength and color, in which all the waves are in step. The beam can be continuous or a series of pulses. Many substances can be stimulated to emit coherent light. Maiman used a ruby crystal, an artificial crystal of aluminum oxide. Neodymium has also been used in lasers, as have liquids including neodymium oxide or neodymium chloride and gases such as carbon monoxide and hydrogen cyanide, as well as a mixture of helium and neon. This mixture was the main substance used in lasers for about 20 years.

ACTIVITIES

First Hand

Theodore H. Maiman: Biographical Memoir
Examine the life of the inventor of the first laser.

1. Is the memoir successful in describing the importance of Maiman and his contribution to science? Justify your conclusions.
2. Why did the *Physical Review* turn down Maiman's first report on his revolutionary laser? Were they shortsighted to do so? Should, as physicist Charles H. Townes states in *Nature* magazine, Maiman's paper be considered the most important of any to appear in that journal for the past 100 years? Why or why not? What effect has the laser had on the modern world?

Weblink

How Lasers Work
Analzye the different types of lasers and how they work.

1. What is the principle behind the laser? Why is laser light different from ordinary visible light?
2. What other uses are there for lasers? How have lasers revolutionized some areas of surgery? Where are they used in everyday life?

Timeline of Science Discoveries

The first half of the twentieth century saw many advances in science and technology being made around the world. These are some of the most important breakthroughs. They cover a wide range of fields of science.

	1910–1915	1915–1920	1920–1925	1925–1930	1930–1935
Technology	**1911** German physicist Ferdinand Brau devises a scanning system for cathode-ray tubes, later used in radar and TV.	**1919** Scottish physicist Robert Watson-Watt patents a short-wave "radiolocator," the forerunner of radar.	**1922** U.S. engineer Lee De Forest creates a sound recording system for movies. **1922** The British Broadcasting Company, or Corporation, begins broadcasts in Britain.	**1926** American inventor Robert Goddard launches a liquid-fuel rocket. **1929** German engineer Felix Wankel patents his rotary engine.	**1930** English engineer Frank Whittle patents the gas turbine, or jet, engine. **1932** U.S. physicist Ernest Lawrence builds the cyclotron, one of the first particle accelerators.
Biology and Medicine	**1913** American geneticist Alfred Sturtevant introduces the technique of chromosome mapping to record the positions of genes along a chromosome.	**1915** English bacteriologist Frederick Twort and French-Canadian Felix d'Hérelle both discover bacteriophages, viruses that can attack bacteria.	**1921** Scottish bacteriologist Alexander Fleming identifies the bacteria-killing enzyme lysozyme.	**1928** Alexander Fleming discovers the antibiotic penicillin. **1929** U.S. chemist Phoebus Levene discovers the sugar deoxyribose in DNA.	**1934** American scientist Royal Raymond Rife tests a cancer-curing treatment using radio waves on human patients.
Physical Sciences	**1913** Danish physicist Niels Bohr proposes his model of the atom, which consists of a central, positively charged nucleus orbited by electrons with negative charges.	**1916** German-born American physicist Albert Einstein publishes his paper on the general theory of relativity, which is mainly concerned with gravity.	**1920** American astronomer Vesto Slipher detects a redshift in the light from galaxies, proving that they are receding and that the Universe is expanding.	**1927** Belgian astronomer Georges Lemaître first proposes what is known as the "big bang" theory of the origin of the Universe.	**1933** Swiss astrophysicist Fritz Zwicky proposes that space must contain invisible "dark matter" to account for the total mass in the Universe.

ACTIVITIES

1935–1940	1940–1945	1945–1950	1950–1955	1955–1960
1935 Scottish physicist Robert Watson-Watt invents radar. **1938** Hungarian-born inventor Laszlo Biró makes a prototype of the first ballpoint pen.	**1942** German rocket engineer Wernher von Braun designs the V-1 and V-2 flying bombs. **1944** U.S. physicist Robert Dicke makes a radiometer to detect microwave radiation.	**1947** U.S. airman "Chuck" Yeager makes the first supersonic flight, in a Bell X-1 airplane. **1949** English computer engineers build EDSAC, an electronic delay-storage automatic calculator.	**1951** U.S. engineers John Mauchly and John Eckert build UNIVAC 1, the first commercial American computer. **1954** Electronics engineer Gordon Teal develops the silicon transistor.	**1956** The world's first commercial nuclear power plant is built at Calder Hall in Great Britain. **1957** Soviet scientists launch the first artificial satellites, Sputnik 1 and Sputnik 2.
1939 U.S. zoologist Victor Shelford introduces the concept of biomes.	**1940** British biochemist Ernst Chain and Australian pathologist Howard Florey extract and purify penicillin, and perform the first clinical trials.	**1945** American biochemist Melvin Calvin begins to study photosynthesis using radioactive carbon-14 as a tracer to follow reactions.	**1952** U.S. physician Jonas Salk develops a vaccine against the polio disease. **1953** Francis Crick, Maurice Wilkins, and James Watson determine the structure of the DNA molecule.	**1958** American microbiologist John Enders produces a vaccine against measles.
1939 French physicists Irène and Frédéric Joliot-Curie show that uranium fission can cause a chain reaction.	**1940** Three new elements are identified—astatine, neptunium, and plutonium. **1942** Italian-American physicist Enrico Fermi achieves the first controlled nuclear chain reaction.	**1949** American pioneer computer engineers John Eckert and John Mauchly construct BINAC, a binary automatic computer.	**1951** American astronomer William Morgan provides evidence that Earth's galaxy, the Milky Way, is a typical spiral galaxy.	**1956** American physicists Clyde Cowan and Frederick Reines discover the neutrino, a subatomic particle with no charge and zero mass.

Transparency

Timeline of Science Discoveries

Analyze important scientific discoveries from 1910 to 1960.

1. What were the major achievements of scientific research in the early twentieth century? What effect did the two world wars have on the process of scientific and technological research? Support your conclusions.
2. Did the inventions or discoveries listed make people's lives better, or did any of them make people's lives worse? Why or why not?

Quiz

1 What was the type of bicycle that replaced the Ordinary?

2 What was the greatest engineering undertaking since the building of the pyramids of Egypt?

3 Who suggested the name proton for the hydrogen nucleus?

4 Which Russian envisioned using rockets to explore space?

5 What new antibiotic helped Allied casualties in World War II?

6 Which Russian-American invented the first workable helicopter?

7 What isotope of uranium is most effective for nuclear fission?

8 What technique did Rosalind Franklin use to begin to decipher the structure of DNA?

9 In which American state is the Very Large Array (VLA)?

10 What kind of crystal did Theodore Maiman use to produce the first laser?

ANSWERS
1. The safety bicycle
2. Building the Panama Canal
3. Ernest Rutherford
4. Konstantin Tsiolkovsky **5.** Penicillin
6. Igor Sikorsky
7. U235 **8.** X-ray diffraction **9.** New Mexico **10.** Ruby

Study the Sources

The history of science is a complicated subject. Historians must be able to understand scientific processes as well as the ways in which history changes because of social, economic, political, or military pressures and opportunities. Adding to the difficulty, the people who recorded advances in the past often did not understand what was actually happening in the scientific developments they were describing.

Consider a major theme discussed in this book. Topics you might choose could be electronics, mass communications, or transportation. Use the internet to find at least two descriptions and at least two images of the topic. Note how people with different viewpoints portrayed different aspects as being important. Some people may be hostile to innovations, while others may be supportive, for example.

Compare the descriptions and images you find with this book. New technology changed many aspects of life. Do you think the historians of the early twentieth century understood the true impact of the changes they recorded? Why do you think it might have been difficult to appreciate developments?

Key Words

Allied: in World War II, relating to the United States, Great Britain, the Soviet Union, and other countries that fought against Germany, Japan, and their allies

anesthetics: substances that cause lack of feeling or awareness

anode: an electrode by which electrons leave an electrical device

bacteria: single-celled organisms that often cause disease

cathode: an electrode by which electrons enter an electrical device

cellulose: the structural component of cell walls in plants, comprising a polymer of glucose units

enzyme: a large protein molecule that enables the chemical reactions on which life depends

heavy water: water in which the hydrogen component is deuterium (2H), or heavy hydrogen, which absorbs neutrons

infrared rays: electromagnetic radiation with frequencies less than visible light and greater than most radio waves

isotopes: atoms of the same element that have the same atomic number but different numbers of neutrons, thus differing in their relative atomic masses

isthmus: a narrow strip of land connecting landmasses, with water on both sides

locks: sets of gates used to raise or lower water level on a canal

magnetic tape: a storage device consisting of a long, thin plastic strip coated with iron oxide

neutron: one of the three main subatomic particles. Neutrons carry no electric charge.

plague: a highly fatal infectious disease caused by bacteria and transmitted through the bite of a rat flea

pneumatic tire: a tire containing air under pressure

polymer: a compound made up of large molecules formed by many smaller molecules combining in a regular pattern

radioactive: describes unstable nuclei that spontaneously decay, emitting alpha particles, beta rays, or gamma rays

radio waves: the part of the electromagnetic spectrum with the longest wavelengths and lowest frequencies. Radio waves are about 100,000 times longer than visible light waves.

repeating gun: a firearm that can fire several rounds before reloading

rotors: spinning blades that achieve lift in the same way as an aircraft wing by creating lower air pressure above the blade than below it

torque: a turning or twisting force

vacuum tube: an airtight glass tube in which electricity is conducted by electrons passing through a partial vacuum from a cathode to an anode

wavelengths: the distances between neighboring peaks or troughs of a traveling wave

X-ray diffraction: the scattering of X-rays by the atoms within a crystal, which produces a diffraction pattern that yields information about the structure of the crystal

Index

LIGHTBOX

SUPPLEMENTARY RESOURCES

Click on the plus icon found in the bottom left corner of each spread to open additional teacher resources.

- Download and print the book's quizzes and activities
- Access curriculum correlations
- Explore additional web applications that enhance the Lightbox experience

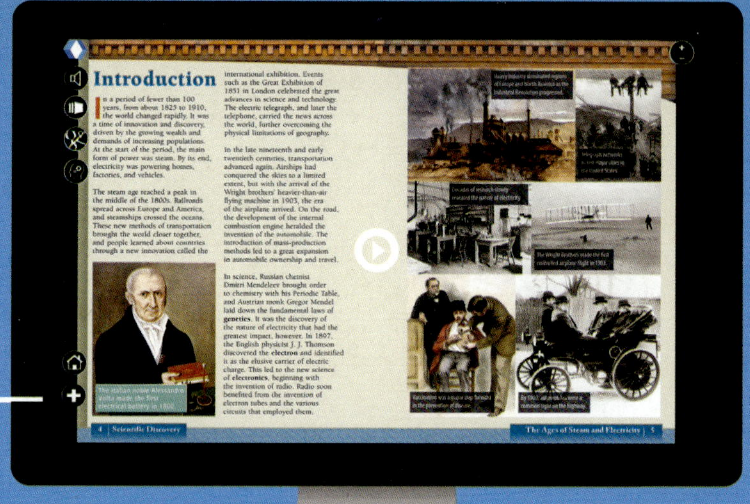

LIGHTBOX DIGITAL TITLES
Packed full of integrated media

VIDEOS

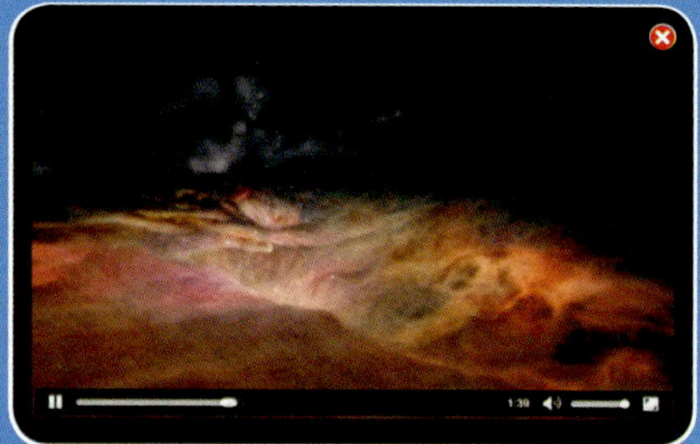

INTERACTIVE MAPS

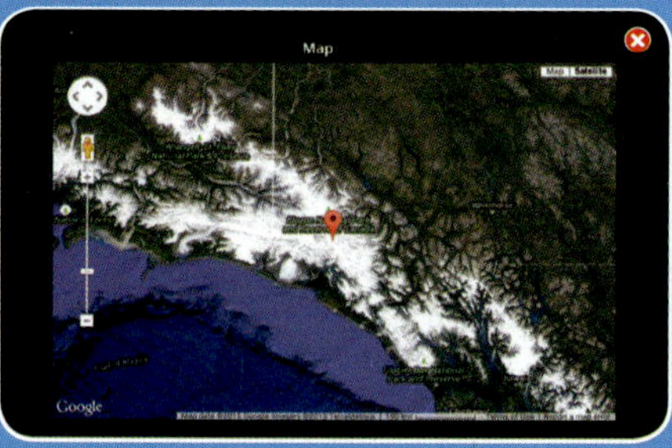

WEBLINKS

SLIDESHOWS

QUIZZES

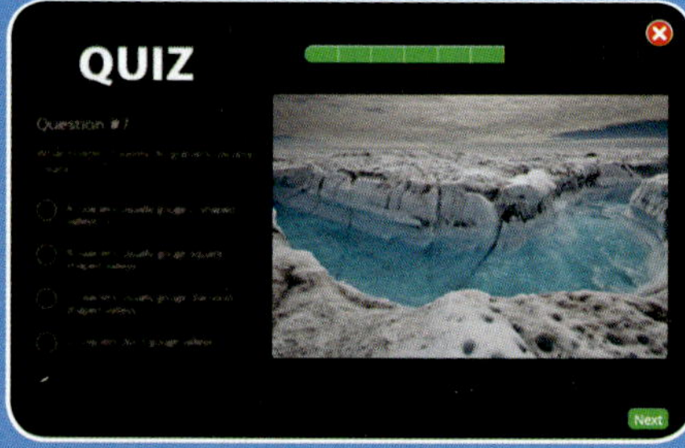

OPTIMIZED FOR
- ✔ TABLETS
- ✔ WHITEBOARDS
- ✔ COMPUTERS
- ✔ AND MUCH MORE!

Published by Smartbook Media Inc.
350 5th Avenue, 59th Floor New York, NY 10118
Website: www.openlightbox.com

First published by Brown Bear Books Limited in 2009

Library of Congress Control Number: 2018941508

ISBN 978-1-5105-3767-5 (hardcover)
ISBN 978-1-5105-3768-2 (multi-user eBook)

Printed in Brainerd, Minnesota, United States
1 2 3 4 5 6 7 8 9 0 22 21 20 19 18

072018
121217

Project Coordinator: Heather Kissock
Art Director: Ana Maria Vidal

Every reasonable effort has been made to trace ownership and to obtain permission to reprint copyright material. The publisher would be pleased to have any errors or omissions brought to its attention so that they may be corrected in subsequent printings.

The publisher acknowledges Getty Images, Alamy, Newscom, Shutterstock, and iStock as its primary image suppliers for this title.